Application for Withholding of Removal and Convention Against Torture

If you have been tortured and/or don't qualify for asylum, CATS might be the relief you should seek in Immigration Court

Attorney Brian D. Lerner

LAW OFFICES OF
BRIAN D. LERNER
A PROFESSIONAL CORPORATION

ATTORNEY DRAFTED IMMIGRATION PETITIONS

By

Brian D. Lerner

Attorney at Law

Disclaimer and Terms of Use:

Effort has been made to ensure that the information in this book is accurate and complete. However, the author and the publisher do not warrant that this particular petition will mirror or be exactly as your situation. There has not been any attorney-client agreement created by the purchase of this petition or application. No legal advice has occurred. The cases, regulations and/or statutes cited may change at any time without notice.

ISBN: 978-1-958990-48-3

INTRODUCTION

There are a multitude of different immigration petitions and applications. They are complex and full of requirements. Obviously, it would be best to hire an immigration attorney to best prepare the petitions and applications. However, this can certainly cost thousands of dollars.

The next best option is to get a sample of the petition written by an experienced immigration attorney. The samples cost a fraction what would be charged by an immigration attorney. However, while the reader has to alter, amend and change the parts of the sample petition to reflect their actual situation, it is a fantastic roadmap for them to use. If the reader has purchased the entire petition or application, they will have real live samples of cover letters, forms, declarations, affidavits and the necessary exhibits to use. The samples come from real cases and the names of those clients have been redacted to protect the privacy of that person or corporation.

These are petitions and applications that have been drafted by an experienced immigration attorney with over 25 years of experience. Get the benefits of that experience without the costs.

CONTENTS

About the Law Offices of Brian D. Lerner

The Law Offices of Brian D. Lerner, APC. The law practice consists of Immigration and Nationality Law and everything involved with and regarding immigration which includes citizenship, investment visas, family and employment visas, removal and deportation hearings, appeals, waivers, adjustment, consulate processing and all types of immigration and citizenship matters. Thousands of families have been reunited and/or permitted to stay in the U.S. and/or return to the U.S. because of the successful work of Immigration Attorney Brian D. Lerner.

This law offices handles all types of immigration cases including family based and employment based. Immigration issues range from immigration court proceedings to trying to fix what paralegals may have done that was neither correct nor proper. Foreign nationals must have experience lawyers admitted to practice law.

The Law Offices of Brian D. Lerner, APC, handles cases arising from business visas, work permits, Green Cards, non-immigrant visas, deportation, citizenship, appeals and all areas of immigration. The Law Offices of Brian D. Lerner, APC does EB-5 Investor Visas, H-1B Specialty Occupation, L-1 Intracompany Transferee, E-2 Treaty Investor, E-1 Treaty Trader, O-1 Extraordinary Ability among others. Regarding immigrant visas for the Green Card, the firm does PERM and advanced degree PERM, Family Petitions, and Extraordinary Alien Petitions. In addition to affirmative petitions, the Law Firm represents people in people in deportation and removal hearings, including political asylum, withholding of removal, and convention against torture cases.

Brian D. Lerner has been certified as an expert in Immigration & Nationality Law by the California State Bar, Board of Legal Specialization since 2000 and has been re-certified three times. He now passes on his decades of experience by allowing the Reader, Law Schools, Professors and other Immigration Attorneys to purchase sample petitions on every facet of Immigration Law.

About the Defense of Asylum Application

Defense of Asylum Application occurs when a request for Asylum as a defense against removal from the U.S. for the Asylum processing to be defensive, the foreign national must be in removal proceedings in immigration court with the Executive Office for Immigration Review (EOIR). First, the Foreign National must establish that they fear persecution in their home country. Secondly, they would be persecuted on account of at least one of five protected grounds: race, religion, nationality, political opinion or particular social group.

I-589 APPLICATION FOR ASYLUM COVER LETTER

Brian D. Lerner (Bar No. 158536)
Christopher A. Reed (Bar No. 235438)
Law Offices of Brian D. Lerner, APC
3233 E. Broadway
Long Beach, CA 90803
Telephone: (562) 495-0554
Facsimile: (562) 608-8672

Attorneys for Respondent

UNITED STATES DEPARTMENT OF JUSTICE

EXECUTIVE OFFICE FOR IMMIGRATION REVIEW

IMMIGRATION COURT

LOS ANGELES, CALIFORNIA

In the Matter of:	
Wuiliam Edgardo CALDERON-ESPINOZA,	File No: 206-897-574
Sandra Liseth LOPEZ DE CALDERON	File No: 206-897-567
Willian Edgardo CALDERON-LOPEZ	File No: 206-897-565
Katherine Rodelmy CALDERON-LOPEZ	File No: 206-897-566
Respondents,	
In Removal Proceedings.	

Immigration Judge: Tara Naselow-Nahas   Master Hearing: March 16, 2016 at 8:30 a.m.

APPLICATION FOR ASYLUM, WITHHOLDING OF REMOVAL AND PROTECTION UNDER THE CONVENTION AGAINST TORTURE

Brian D. Lerner (Bar No. 158536)
Christopher A. Reed (Bar No. 235438)
Law Offices of Brian D. Lerner, APC
3233 E. Broadway
Long Beach, CA 90803
Telephone: (562) 495-0554
Facsimile: (562) 608-8672

Attorneys for Respondent

NON-DETAINED

UNITED STATES DEPARTMENT OF JUSTICE

EXECUTIVE OFFICE FOR IMMIGRATION REVIEW

IMMIGRATION COURT

LOS ANGELES, CALIFORNIA

In the Matter of: Wuiliam Edgardo CALDERON-ESPINOZA, Sandra Liseth LOPEZ DE CALDERON Willian Edgardo CALDERON-LOPEZ Katherine Rodelmy CALDERON-LOPEZ Respondents, In Removal Proceedings.	File No: 206-897-574 File No: 206-897-567 File No: 206-897-565 File No: 206-897-566

Immigration Judge: Hye Y. Chon

Master Hearing: August 5, 2019 at 8:30 a.m.

SUPPLEMENTAL DOCUMENTS FOR APPLICATION FOR ASYLUM, WITHHOLDING OF REMOVAL AND PROTECTION UNDER THE CONVENTION AGAINST TORTURE

I-589 APPLICATION FOR ASYLUM FOR WITHHOLDING OF REMOVAL AND RECEIPT NOTICE

Department of Homeland Security
U.S. Citizenship and Immigration Services

U.S. Department of Justice
Executive Office for Immigration Review

OMB No. 1615-0067; Expires 12/31/2016

I-589, Application for Asylum and for Withholding of Removal

START HERE - Type or print in black ink. See the instructions for information about eligibility and how to complete and file this application. There is NO filing fee for this application.

NOTE: Check this box if you also want to apply for withholding of removal under the Convention Against Torture. [X]

Part A.I. Information About You

1. Alien Registration Number(s) (A-Number) *(if any)* 206-897-574		2. U.S. Social Security Number *(if any)* N/A	
3. Complete Last Name CALDERON-ESPINOZA	4. First Name Wuiliam	5. Middle Name Edgardo	
6. What other names have you used *(include maiden name and aliases)*?			
7. Residence in the U.S. *(where you physically reside)*			
Street Number and Name 7815 S. San Pedro Street		Apt. Number	
City Los Angeles	State CA	Zip Code 90003	Telephone Number (323) 531-2089
8. Mailing Address in the U.S. *(if different than the address in Item Number 7)*			
In Care Of *(if applicable)*:		Telephone Number	
Street Number and Name		Apt. Number	
City	State	Zip Code	
9. Gender: [X] Male [ ] Female	10. Marital Status: [ ] Single [X] Married [ ] Divorced [ ] Widowed		
11. Date of Birth *(mm/dd/yyyy)* 06/11/1979	12. City and Country of Birth Ahuchapan El Salvador		
13. Present Nationality *(Citizenship)* El Salvador	14. Nationality at Birth Salvadorian	15. Race, Ethnic, or Tribal Group Latino	16. Religion Christian; Evangelical

17. *Check the box, a through c, that applies:* a. [ ] I have never been in Immigration Court proceedings.
b. [X] I am now in Immigration Court proceedings. c. [ ] I am **not** now in Immigration Court proceedings, but I have been in the past.

18. *Complete 18 a through c.*

a. When did you last leave your country? *(mmm/dd/yyyy)* 01/23/2015 b. What is your current I-94 Number, if any? N/A

c. List each entry into the U.S. beginning with your most recent entry. *List date (mm/dd/yyyy), place, and your status for each entry. (Attach additional sheets as needed.)*

Date	Place	Status	Date Status Expires
02/10/2015	Hidalgo, TX	EWI	

19. What country issued your last passport or travel document? El Salvador	20. Passport Number A01285485 / Travel Document Number N/A	21. Expiration Date *(mm/dd/yyyy)*
22. What is your native language *(include dialect, if applicable)*? Spanish	23. Are you fluent in English? [ ] Yes [X] No	24. What other languages do you speak fluently? N/A

For EOIR use only.	**For USCIS use only.** **Action:** Interview Date: ____ Asylum Officer ID#: ____	**Decision:** Approval Date: ____ Denial Date: ____ Referral Date: ____

DEPARTMENT OF JUSTICE EXECUTIVE OFFICE FOR IMMIGRATION REVIEW IMMIGRATION COURT LOS ANGELES, CA — LODGED NOT FILED

RECEIVED ... JAN 20 ... 10:48

Form I-589 (Rev. 12/29/14) Y

4415

Part A.II. Information About Your Spouse and Children

Your spouse ☐ I am not married. (Skip to Your Children below.)

1. Alien Registration Number (A-Number) *(if any)*	2. Passport/ID Card Number *(if any)*	3. Date of Birth *(mm/dd/yyyy)*	4. U.S. Social Security Number *(if any)*
206-897-567	A01400975	07/08/1980	N/A
5. Complete Last Name	**6. First Name**	**7. Middle Name**	**8. Maiden Name**
LOPEZ DE CALDERON	Sandra	Liseth	LOPEZ
9. Date of Marriage *(mm/dd/yyyy)*	**10. Place of Marriage**	**11. City and Country of Birth**	
02/09/2001	Colon, El Salvador	Santa Isabel Ishuatan El Salvador	
12. Nationality *(Citizenship)*	**13. Race, Ethnic, or Tribal Group**	**14. Gender**	
Salvadorian	Latina	☐ Male ☒ Female	
15. Is this person in the U.S.?	☒ Yes *(Complete Blocks 16 to 24.)* ☐ No *(Specify location):*		
16. Place of last entry into the U.S.	**17. Date of last entry into the U.S.** *(mm/dd/yyyy)*	**18. I-94 Number** *(if any)*	**19. Status when last admitted** *(Visa type, if any)*
Hidalgo, TX	02/10/2015	N/A	EWI
20. What is your spouse's current status?	**21. What is the expiration date of his/her authorized stay, if any?** *(mm/dd/yyyy)*	**22. Is your spouse in Immigration Court proceedings?**	**23. If previously in the U.S., date of previous arrival** *(mm/dd/yyyy)*
Out of Status		☒ Yes ☐ No	

24. If in the U.S., is your spouse to be included in this application? *(Check the appropriate box.)*

☒ Yes *(Attach one photograph of your spouse in the upper right corner of Page 9 on the extra copy of the application submitted for this person.)*

☐ No

Your Children. List all of your children, regardless of age, location, or marital status.

☐ I do not have any children. *(Skip to Part A.III., **Information about your background.**)*

☒ I have children. Total number of children: 2

(**NOTE:** *Use Form I-589 Supplement A or attach additional sheets of paper and documentation if you have more than four children.*)

1. Alien Registration Number (A-Number) *(if any)*	2. Passport/ID Card Number *(if any)*	3. Marital Status *(Married, Single, Divorced, Widowed)*	4. U.S. Social Security Number *(if any)*
206-897-566	N/A	Single	N/A
5. Complete Last Name	**6. First Name**	**7. Middle Name**	**8. Date of Birth** *(mm/dd/yyyy)*
CALDERON-LOPEZ	Katherine	Rodelmy	04/24/2001
9. City and Country of Birth	**10. Nationality** *(Citizenship)*	**11. Race, Ethnic, or Tribal Group**	**12. Gender**
Santa Isabel Ishuatan El Salvador	Salvadorian	Latina	☐ Male ☒ Female
13. Is this child in the U.S.?	☒ Yes *(Complete Blocks 14 to 21.)* ☐ No *(Specify location):*		
14. Place of last entry into the U.S.	**15. Date of last entry into the U.S.** *(mm/dd/yyyy)*	**16. I-94 Number** *(If any)*	**17. Status when last admitted** *(Visa type, if any)*
Hidalgo, TX	02/10/2015	N/A	EWI
18. What is your child's current status?	**19. What is the expiration date of his/her authorized stay, if any?** *(mm/dd/yyyy)*	**20. Is your child in Immigration Court proceedings?**	
Out of Status		☒ Yes ☐ No	

21. If in the U.S., is this child to be included in this application? *(Check the appropriate box.)*

☒ Yes *(Attach one photograph of your spouse in the upper right corner of Page 9 on the extra copy of the application submitted for this person.)*

☐ No

Part A.II. Information About Your Spouse and Children (Continued)

1. Alien Registration Number (A-Number) *(if any)* 206-897-565	2. Passport/ID Card Number *(if any)* N/A	3. Marital Status *(Married, Single, Divorced, Widowed)* Single	4. U.S. Social Security Number *(if any)* N/A
5. Complete Last Name CALDERON-LOPEZ	6. First Name Willian	7. Middle Name Edgardo	8. Date of Birth *(mm/dd/yyyy)* 06/29/2007
9. City and Country of Birth Colon El Salvador	10. Nationality *(Citizenship)* Salvadorian	11. Race, Ethnic, or Tribal Group Latino	12. Gender ☒ Male ☐ Female
13. Is this child in the U.S. ? ☒ Yes *(Complete Blocks 14 to 21.)* ☐ No *(Specify location):*			
14. Place of last entry into the U.S. Hidalgo, TX	15. Date of last entry into the U.S. *(mm/dd/yyyy)* 02/10/2015	16. I-94 Number *(If any)* N/A	17. Status when last admitted *(Visa type, if any)* EWI
18. What is your child's current status? Out of Status	19. What is the expiration date of his/her authorized stay, if any? *(mm/dd/yyyy)*	20. Is your child in Immigration Court proceedings? ☒ Yes ☐ No	
21. If in the U.S., is this child to be included in this application? *(Check the appropriate box.)* ☒ Yes *(Attach one photograph of your spouse in the upper right corner of Page 9 on the extra copy of the application submitted for this person.)* ☐ No			

1. Alien Registration Number (A-Number) *(if any)*	2. Passport/ID Card Number *(if any)*	3. Marital Status *(Married, Single, Divorced, Widowed)* -	4. U.S. Social Security Number *(if any)*
5. Complete Last Name	6. First Name	7. Middle Name	8. Date of Birth *(mm/dd/yyyy)*
9. City and Country of Birth	10. Nationality *(Citizenship)*	11. Race, Ethnic, or Tribal Group	12. Gender ☐ Male ☐ Female
13. Is this child in the U.S. ? ☐ Yes *(Complete Blocks 14 to 21.)* ☐ No *(Specify location):*			
14. Place of last entry into the U.S.	15. Date of last entry into the U.S. *(mm/dd/yyyy)*	16. I-94 Number *(If any)*	17. Status when last admitted *(Visa type, if any)*
18. What is your child's current status?	19. What is the expiration date of his/her authorized stay, if any? *(mm/dd/yyyy)*	20. Is your child in Immigration Court proceedings? ☐ Yes ☐ No	
21. If in the U.S., is this child to be included in this application? *(Check the appropriate box.)* ☐ Yes *(Attach one photograph of your spouse in the upper right corner of Page 9 on the extra copy of the application submitted for this person.)* ☐ No			

1. Alien Registration Number (A-Number) *(if any)*	2. Passport/ID Card Number *(if any)*	3. Marital Status *(Married, Single, Divorced, Widowed)* -	4. U.S. Social Security Number *(if any)*
5. Complete Last Name	6. First Name	7. Middle Name	8. Date of Birth *(mm/dd/yyyy)*
9. City and Country of Birth	10. Nationality *(Citizenship)*	11. Race, Ethnic, or Tribal Group	12. Gender ☐ Male ☐ Female
13. Is this child in the U.S. ? ☐ Yes *(Complete Blocks 14 to 21.)* ☐ No *(Specify location):*			
14. Place of last entry into the U.S.	15. Date of last entry into the U.S. *(mm/dd/yyyy)*	16. I-94 Number *(If any)*	17. Status when last admitted *(Visa type, if any)*
18. What is your child's current status?	19. What is the expiration date of his/her authorized stay, if any? *(mm/dd/yyyy)*	20. Is your child in Immigration Court proceedings? ☐ Yes ☐ No	
21. If in the U.S., is this child to be included in this application? *(Check the appropriate box.)* ☐ Yes *(Attach one photograph of your spouse in the upper right corner of Page 9 on the extra copy of the application submitted for this person.)* ☐ No			

Part A.III. Information About Your Background

1. List your last address where you lived before coming to the United States. If this is not the country where you fear persecution, also list the last address in the country where you fear persecution. *(List Address, City/Town, Department, Province, or State and Country.)*
(**NOTE:** *Use Form I-589 Supplement B, or additional sheets of paper, if necessary.)*

Number and Street *(Provide if available)*	City/Town	Department, Province, or State	Country	Dates From *(Mo/Yr)*	To *(Mo/Yr)*
Colonia el Pital Pasejo J No. 10	Colon	Lourdes	El Salvador	02 2001	01 2015

2. Provide the following information about your residences during the past 5 years. List your present address first.
(**NOTE:** *Use Form I-589 Supplement B, or additional sheets of paper, if necessary.)*

Number and Street	City/Town	Department, Province, or State	Country	Dates From *(Mo/Yr)*	To *(Mo/Yr)*
7815 S. San Pedro Street	Los Angeles	CA	USA	02 2015	
Colonia el Pital Pasejo J No. 10	Colon	Lourdes	El Salvador	02 2001	01 2015

3. Provide the following information about your education, beginning with the most recent.
(**NOTE:** *Use Form I-589 Supplement B, or additional sheets of paper, if necessary.)*

Name of School	Type of School	Location *(Address)*	Attended From *(Mo/Yr)*	To *(Mo/Yr)*
ITCA	Technical University	Santa Tecla, El Salvador	01 1998	01 1999
Nuevo Liceo Centro Americano	College	Decima Avenida Sur, San Salvador, El Salvador	01 1995	01 1997

4. Provide the following information about your employment during the past 5 years. List your present employment first.
(**NOTE:** *Use Form I-589 Supplement B, or additional sheets of paper, if necessary.)*

Name and Address of Employer	Your Occupation	Dates From *(Mo/Yr)*	To *(Mo/Yr)*
ANDA Ave. Don Bosco Colon la Libertad, Edificio Anda	Electrician	01 2002	01 2015

5. Provide the following information about your parents and siblings (brothers and sisters). Check the box if the person is deceased.
(**NOTE:** *Use Form I-589 Supplement B, or additional sheets of paper, if necessary.)*

	Full Name	City/Town and Country of Birth	Current Location
Mother	ESPINOZA Martha Erolda	Juayua El Salvador	☐ Deceased Sonsonate El Salvador
Father	CALDERON HIDALGO Francisco Irene	Ahuachapan El Salvador	☐ Deceased Sonsonate El Salvador
Sibling	CALDERON Fredy Yovani	Ahuachapan El Salvador	☐ Deceased Colon la Libertad El Salvador
Sibling	CALDERSON Besi [illegible]	Ahuachapan El Salvador	☐ Deceased Sonsonate El Salvador
Sibling	CALDERON Jaime Francisco	Sonsonate El Salvador	☐ Deceased Sonsonate El Salvador
Sibling	CALDERON Victor Manuel	Sonsonate El Salvador	☐ Deceased Sonsonate El Salvador
	CALDERON [illegible]	Sonsonate El Sal	Santa Tecla

Part B. Information About Your Application

(NOTE: *Use Form I-589 Supplement B, or attach additional sheets of paper as needed to complete your responses to the questions contained in Part B.)*

When answering the following questions about your asylum or other protection claim (withholding of removal under 241(b)(3) of the INA or withholding of removal under the Convention Against Torture), you must provide a detailed and specific account of the basis of your claim to asylum or other protection. To the best of your ability, provide specific dates, places, and descriptions about each event or action described. You must attach documents evidencing the general conditions in the country from which you are seeking asylum or other protection and the specific facts on which you are relying to support your claim. If this documentation is unavailable or you are not providing this documentation with your application, explain why in your responses to the following questions.

Refer to Instructions, Part 1: Filing Instructions, Section II, "Basis of Eligibility," Parts A - D, Section V, "Completing the Form," Part B, and Section VII, "Additional Evidence That You Should Submit," for more information on completing this section of the form.

1. Why are you applying for asylum or withholding of removal under section 241(b)(3) of the INA, or for withholding of removal under the Convention Against Torture? Check the appropriate box(es) below and then provide detailed answers to questions A and B below.

I am seeking asylum or withholding of removal based on:

- ☐ Race
- ☐ Religion
- ☐ Nationality
- ☐ Political opinion
- ☒ Membership in a particular social group
- ☒ Torture Convention

A. Have you, your family, or close friends or colleagues ever experienced harm or mistreatment or threats in the past by anyone?

☐ No ☒ Yes

If "Yes," explain in detail:
1. What happened;
2. When the harm or mistreatment or threats occurred;
3. Who caused the harm or mistreatment or threats; and
4. Why you believe the harm or mistreatment or threats occurred.

My family and I were threatened on several occasions in El Salvador. On one occasion on December 31, 2014, we were walking home from church when 4 masked individuals approached us and demanded money from us. One of the men grabbed my daughter and when I tired to help her, the other men pushed me to the ground and began beating me.

Two of my sister-in-law's sisters were also kidnapped, raped and murdered.

See attached declaration.

B. Do you fear harm or mistreatment if you return to your home country?

☐ No ☒ Yes

If "Yes," explain in detail:
1. What harm or mistreatment you fear;
2. Who you believe would harm or mistreat you; and
3. Why you believe you would or could be harmed or mistreated.

Because of the incidents described above, I fear that my family and I will be killed if we are forced to return to El Salvador.

Part B. Information About Your Application (Continued)

2. Have you or your family members ever been accused, charged, arrested, detained, interrogated, convicted and sentenced, or imprisoned in any country other than the United States?

☒ No ☐ Yes

If "Yes," explain the circumstances and reasons for the action.

3.A. Have you or your family members ever belonged to or been associated with any organizations or groups in your home country, such as, but not limited to, a political party, student group, labor union, religious organization, military or paramilitary group, civil patrol, guerrilla organization, ethnic group, human rights group, or the press or media?

☐ No ☒ Yes

If "Yes," describe for each person the level of participation, any leadership or other positions held, and the length of time you or your family members were involved in each organization or activity.

My family and I are Christians and we were members of the church in El Salvador - Tabernáculo Biblico Bautista Amigos de Israel. We went to church several times a week and would also travel to other cities to worship.

3.B. Do you or your family members continue to participate in any way in these organizations or groups?

☐ No ☒ Yes

If "Yes," describe for each person your or your family members' current level of participation, any leadership or other positions currently held, and the length of time you or your family members have been involved in each organization or group.

4. Are you afraid of being subjected to torture in your home country or any other country to which you may be returned?

☐ No ☒ Yes

If "Yes," explain why you are afraid and describe the nature of torture you fear, by whom, and why it would be inflicted.

Because of the incidents described above, I fear that my family and I will be killed if we are forced to return to El Salvador.

Part C. Additional Information About Your Application

(**NOTE:** *Use Form I-589 Supplement B, or attach additional sheets of paper as needed to complete your responses to the questions contained in Part C.*)

1. Have you, your spouse, your child(ren), your parents or your siblings ever applied to the U.S. Government for refugee status, asylum, or withholding of removal?

[X] No [ ] Yes

If "Yes," explain the decision and what happened to any status you, your spouse, your child(ren), your parents, or your siblings received as a result of that decision. Indicate whether or not you were included in a parent or spouse's application. If so, include your parent or spouse's A-number in your response. If you have been denied asylum by an immigration judge or the Board of Immigration Appeals, describe any change(s) in conditions in your country or your own personal circumstances since the date of the denial that may affect your eligibility for asylum.

2.A. After leaving the country from which you are claiming asylum, did you or your spouse or child(ren) who are now in the United States travel through or reside in any other country before entering the United States?

[ ] No [X] Yes

2.B. Have you, your spouse, your child(ren), or other family members, such as your parents or siblings, ever applied for or received any lawful status in any country other than the one from which you are now claiming asylum?

[X] No [ ] Yes

If "Yes" to either or both questions (2A and/or 2B), provide for each person the following: the name of each country and the length of stay, the person's status while there, the reasons for leaving, whether or not the person is entitled to return for lawful residence purposes, and whether the person applied for refugee status or for asylum while there, and if not, why he or she did not do so.

My family and I travelled through Guatemala and Mexico on our way to the United States.

3. Have you, your spouse or your child(ren) ever ordered, incited, assisted or otherwise participated in causing harm or suffering to any person because of his or her race, religion, nationality, membership in a particular social group or belief in a particular political opinion?

[X] No [ ] Yes

If "Yes," describe in detail each such incident and your own, your spouse's, or your child(ren)'s involvement.

Part C. Additional Information About Your Application (Continued)

4. After you left the country where you were harmed or fear harm, did you return to that country?

☒ No ☐ Yes

If "Yes," describe in detail the circumstances of your visit(s) (for example, the date(s) of the trip(s), the purpose(s) of the trip(s), and the length of time you remained in that country for the visit(s).)

5. Are you filing this application more than 1 year after your last arrival in the United States?

☐ No ☒ Yes

If "Yes," explain why you did not file within the first year after you arrived. You must be prepared to explain at your interview or hearing why you did not file your asylum application within the first year after you arrived. For guidance in answering this question, see Instructions, Part 1: Filing Instructions, Section V. "Completing the Form," Part C.

My case was consolidated with my family's cases and my first hearing was not scheduled until after the 1 year filing deadline. My motion to advance was denied by the Court but the Court found an exception to the 1 year filing deadline. I also lodged my application with the Court prior to the 1 year deadline.

6. Have you or any member of your family included in the application ever committed any crime and/or been arrested, charged, convicted, or sentenced for any crimes in the United States?

☒ No ☐ Yes

If "Yes," for each instance, specify in your response: what occurred and the circumstances, dates, length of sentence received, location, the duration of the detention or imprisonment, reason(s) for the detention or conviction, any formal charges that were lodged against you or your relatives included in your application, and the reason(s) for release. Attach documents referring to these incidents, if they are available, or an explanation of why documents are not available.

Part D. Your Signature

I certify, under penalty of perjury under the laws of the United States of America, that this application and the evidence submitted with it are all true and correct. Title 18, United States Code, Section 1546(a), provides in part: Whoever knowingly makes under oath, or as permitted under penalty of perjury under Section 1746 of Title 28, United States Code, knowingly subscribes as true, any false statement with respect to a material fact in any application, affidavit, or other document required by the immigration laws or regulations prescribed thereunder, or knowingly presents any such application, affidavit, or other document containing any such false statement or which fails to contain any reasonable basis in law or fact - shall be fined in accordance with this title or imprisoned for up to 25 years. I authorize the release of any information from my immigration record that U.S. Citizenship and Immigration Services (USCIS) needs to determine eligibility for the benefit I am seeking.

Staple your photograph here or the photograph of the family member to be included on the extra copy of the application submitted for that person.

WARNING: **Applicants who are in the United States illegally are subject to removal if their asylum or withholding claims are not granted by an asylum officer or an immigration judge. Any information provided in completing this application may be used as a basis for the institution of, or as evidence in, removal proceedings even if the application is later withdrawn. Applicants determined to have knowingly made a frivolous application for asylum will be permanently ineligible for any benefits under the Immigration and Nationality Act. You may not avoid a frivolous finding simply because someone advised you to provide false information in your asylum application. If filing with USCIS, unexcused failure to appear for an appointment to provide biometrics (such as fingerprints) and your biographical information within the time allowed may result in an asylum officer dismissing your asylum application or referring it to an immigration judge. Failure without good cause to provide DHS with biometrics or other biographical information while in removal proceedings may result in your application being found abandoned by the immigration judge. See sections 208(d)(5)(A) and 208(d)(6) of the INA and 8 CFR sections 208.10, 1208.10, 208.20, 1003.47(d) and 1208.20.**

Print your complete name.	Write your name in your native alphabet.
Wuiliam Edgardo CALDERON-ESPINOZA	

Did your spouse, parent, or child(ren) assist you in completing this application? ☒ No ☐ Yes *(If "Yes," list the name and relationship.)*

(Name) *(Relationship)* *(Name)* *(Relationship)*

Did someone other than your spouse, parent, or child(ren) prepare this application? ☐ No ☒ Yes *(If "Yes," complete Part E.)*

Asylum applicants may be represented by counsel. Have you been provided with a list of persons who may be available to assist you, at little or no cost, with your asylum claim? ☐ No ☒ Yes

Signature of Applicant *(The person in Part A.I.)*

[ ]

Sign your name so it all appears within the brackets

12/09/2015

Date *(mm/dd/yyyy)*

Part E. Declaration of Person Preparing Form, if Other Than Applicant, Spouse, Parent, or Child

I declare that I have prepared this application at the request of the person named in Part D, that the responses provided are based on all information of which I have knowledge, or which was provided to me by the applicant, and that the completed application was read to the applicant in his or her native language or a language he or she understands for verification before he or she signed the application in my presence. I am aware that the knowing placement of false information on the Form I-589 may also subject me to civil penalties under 8 U.S.C. 1324c and/or criminal penalties under 18 U.S.C. 1546(a).

Signature of Preparer	Print Complete Name of Preparer		
	Christopher A. Reed		
Daytime Telephone Number: (562) 495-0554	Address of Preparer: Street Number and Name: 3233 E. Broadway		
Apt. Number	City: Long Beach	State: CA	Zip Code: 90803

Part F. To Be Completed at Asylum Interview, if Applicable

NOTE: *You will be asked to complete this part when you appear for examination before an asylum officer of the Department of Homeland Security, U.S. Citizenship and Immigration Services (USCIS).*

I swear (affirm) that I know the contents of this application that I am signing, including the attached documents and supplements, that they are ☐ all true or ☐ not all true to the best of my knowledge and that correction(s) numbered ____ to ____ were made by me or at my request. Furthermore, I am aware that if I am determined to have knowingly made a frivolous application for asylum I will be permanently ineligible for any benefits under the Immigration and Nationality Act, and that I may not avoid a frivolous finding simply because someone advised me to provide false information in my asylum application.

Signed and sworn to before me by the above named applicant on:

Signature of Applicant	Date *(mm/dd/yyyy)*
Write Your Name in Your Native Alphabet	Signature of Asylum Officer

Part G. To Be Completed at Removal Hearing, if Applicable

NOTE: *You will be asked to complete this Part when you appear before an immigration judge of the U.S. Department of Justice, Executive Office for Immigration Review (EOIR), for a hearing.*

I swear (affirm) that I know the contents of this application that I am signing, including the attached documents and supplements, that they are ☐ all true or ☐ not all true to the best of my knowledge and that correction(s) numbered ____ to ____ were made by me or at my request. Furthermore, I am aware that if I am determined to have knowingly made a frivolous application for asylum I will be permanently ineligible for any benefits under the Immigration and Nationality Act, and that I may not avoid a frivolous finding simply because someone advised me to provide false information in my asylum application.

Signed and sworn to before me by the above named applicant on:

Signature of Applicant	Date *(mm/dd/yyyy)*
Write Your Name in Your Native Alphabet	Signature of Immigration Judge

FROM

US DEPT OF HOMELAND [illegible] URITY
USCIS Nebraska Serv[illegible] Center
Defens[illegible] Appl. With Immigr Court
P.O. BOX 87597
[illegible]NCOLN, NE 68501-[illegible]

NAME [illegible] CALDERON ESPINOZA DATE 10/06/15
A NUMBER [illegible] RCPT# [illegible] FORM I589
*** ACKNOWLEDGEMENT OF RECEIPT ***
USCIS has received a copy of your I-589 (application for Asylum and Withholding of Removal) filed in defense of removal from the US in Immigration Court. Pursuant to S.265 of the Immigration and Nationality Act, you are required to notify USCIS, in writing, of any address changes, within 10 days of such change using Form AR11. Since you were placed in removal proceedings before an Immigration Judge, you are also required to notify the Immigration Court having jurisdiction over your case of any change [illegible] [illegible] [illegible] changed [illegible] [illegible] AR11 and [illegible] the location specified on the [illegible] form.

TO

CHRISTOPHER REED
C/O LAW OFFICES OF BRIAN [illegible] LERNER
[illegible] E BROADWAY

LONG BEACH, CA [illegible]

EXHIBITS

EXHIBIT '1':
Declaration of Wuiliam Edgardo Calderon-Espinoza

ENGLISH TRANSLATION OF SPANISH DECLARATION

DECLARATION OF WUILIAM EDGARDO CALDERON-ESPINOZA

1. I, Wuiliam Edgardo Calderon Espinoza, was born on June 11, 1979, in Ahuachapán, El Salvador.

2. I entered the United States on February 10, 2015 through Hidalgo, Texas, without inspection. With me entered my wife and two children. Since our entry we have not left the country.

3. I am married to Sandra Liseth Lopez Calderon. We have two children. Katherine Calderon Lopez Rodelmy 14 years old and Willian Edgardo Lopez Calderon 8 years old.

4. In August 2010, I received a call from number 72611317. They called me by my name, I was told not to hang up or I would regret it. I asked them who they were. They told me not to hang up because they were watching me. They told me the names of all members of my family. They also told me where my daughter studied. They also told me if I did not follow their orders and deliver what they were asking for, my family would pay the consequences. They said I would need to give them $2,000 and had only 4 days to deliver the money, because if I did not deliver the money, they would kill my parents. I replied that I had no money, but they told me, but if you work in ANDA (National Administration of Aqueducts and Sewers) we know you have money, it is an order and do not say anything to the police, or anyone, because we have contacts and we will be notified if you put a complaint. They said you know what our motto is, "Death to informers." These people who called me are known as MS-13 aka Terrorists in El Salvador.

5. The next day they called me, I was told to leave the money on the left corner of "Cancha de los Olivos," (which is an abandoned lot), and that if I followed orders everything would be fine. With much fear I took the money and did not hear anything more.

6. After 6 months, two armed people came to my house, they told me because of my job that I had to pay them $25 dollars a week, it's an order they told me. I was told that if I did not pay, they would be kill me.

7. With great effort I was paying this amount for many years. They went to collect this money every Saturday; at any time to my house. They would knock at the door and I would give them the money. Every Saturday I would stay at home waiting for them. Every time it was different people who would collect the money, that was always given to them in cash. I gave them this money from 2011 until January 2015, when we decided to leave the country.

8. On December 20, 2014, again they came to my house armed and covered their faces similar to the way police officers are uniformed in my country. They pushed the door and got in by force, they said they would change the laws of the city. That I would no longer be paying $25 dollars to them but instead it would go up to $500 dollars a month. These people told me since I was employed by ANDA, and had a very good monthly salary of $695 dollars a month, I would have to pay this

\

amount and that I had to pay immediately. These people threatened me with raping my wife and daughter, in person when they went to collect the money. At that time I only had $300 dollars, and they told me to get ready with the rest of the money, if I did not then, I would know what will happen to my wife and daughter. We will ape them and kill them in front of you. I was also told that if I did not continue paying them they would kill me, and that our lives depended on the money I had to pay them. I was again threatened, they told me not to move, because wherever I would move to they would find me and were going to torture me. They also said they would do the same thing they did to the Valladares (they were my brother's sister in laws that were kidnapped, raped and then found in a clandestine cemetery after six months).

9. On December 31, we were coming from church my children walked about 200 feet away from me and out of the darkness of the night four men appeared out of nowhere. One of them grabbed my daughter, my daughter then yelled for me. I ran to help her I was grabbed by 3 men that began to hit me, I wanted defend myself but I was outnumbered. I fell into the ditch and these men continue to beat me, they kicked me.. The man who had my daughter let her go. With a gun in hand they threatened me and continued to beat me. With the gun a man hit me on my forehead, I did not know who he was they had their faces covered, they told me they would kill me there. My wife and son were asking them not kill me. Then they left me, I think it was because my family were pleading for them to spare my life, but I was told that this was just a warning. I was also told that if I did not continue to pay them, or if I were to make a report to the police, or that if I moved, my daughter and wife were going to get raped and then killed. They told me remember what happened to your brother's sister in laws and that the same thing was going to happen to us.

10. That night we decided go to another town called Sonsonate, Canton Mira Valles, Dept which is three hours from where we lived, and stayed with my father, because we were afraid they would return to kill us. My daughter was crying and told me that the guy who grabbed, touched her breasts and tried to touch her private parts. My daughter was and still afraid that they will rape her. Out of fear we had to leave everything we had in our home.

11. On January 19, 2015, my wife received another call, they told her that they already had permission to kill us. The person told her since we had not given the money and we moved "we're going to bust your ass." Also they told her that they were already notifying all their contacts. They sent us a text message where it said that if my wife were seen outside they were going smash her anus, and they were going to pierce her chest with bullets. Because no one mocked them, and escaped from them. They also said they would find us wherever we went and were going to kill us. So we had no option but to leave our country.

12. We never reported any of these threats because of the fear that these people would not only kill us but our parents as well. Also because these people know people within the police system, as they told me several times when they threatened me.

13. Since we left our country, the last thing I found out is that these people burglarized everything that was in my house. I want clarify that they are categorized as "terrorists," they are different from the "Maras."

14. For these reasons, not only myself but my wife and children are afraid to return to our country. If we were to go back to El Salvador, for sure they we kill us, because these people think that we made a mockery out of them, we have much fear of returning.

I declare under penalty of perjury under the laws of the State of California that the foregoing is true and correct. Executed in Long Beach, California

Date:.______________________ ______________________________

Wuiliam Edgardo CALDERON-ESPINOZA

Translator's Certificate of Competence

I, Tanya Stewart, certify that the above is an accurate translation of the original Declaration of Wuiliam Calderon-Espinoza in Spanish and that I am competent in both English and Spanish to render such translation.

Tanya Stewart 03.15.2016

Tanya Stewart Date

Law Offices of Brian D. Lerner
3233 East Broadway
Long Beach, CA 90803
Tel: (562) 495-0554

DECLARACIÓN DE WUILIAM EDGARDO CALDERON-ESPINOZA

1. Yo, Wuiliam Edgardo Calderon Espinoza, naci el dia 11 de Junio de 1979, en Ahuachapán, El Salvador.

2. Entre a los Estados Unidos el día 10 de Febrero de 2015 por Hidalgo, Texas, sin inspección. Conmigo entraron mi esposa y mis dos hijos. Desde nuestra entrada no hemos salido de el país.

3. Yo estoy casado con Sandra Liseth Lopez de Calderon. Tenemos dos hijos: Katherine Rodelmy Calderon Lopez de 14 años y Willian Edgardo Calderon Lopez de 8 anos.

4. En Agosto del 2010 recibí una llamada del numero 72611317. Me llamaron por mi nombre, me dijeron que no colgara si no me arrepentiría. Yo les pregunte quien eran. Ellos me dijeron que no colgara porque me tenían vigilado. Me dijeron los nombres de todos los miembros de mi familia. También me dijeron en donde estudiaba mi hija. Ellos también me dijeron que si no siguió las órdenes y entregará lo que me iban a pedir, mi familia pagaria las consequencias. Me dijeron que iban a necesitar que les diera $2,000 dolares y que tenia solo 4 dias para entregarlo, porque si no lo entregaba iban a matar a mis padres. Yo le conteste que no tenía dinero, pero ellos me dijeron pero si trabajas en ANDA (Administración Nacional de Acueductos y Alcantarillados) sabemos que tienes dinero, es una orden y no digas nada a la policía, ni a nadien porque tenemos contactos y nos van a avisar si pones denuncia. Me dijeron sabes cual es el lema de nosotros, "Muerte a los soplones." Estas personas que me llamaron son conocidos como MS-13 aka Terroristas en el Salvador.

5. El dia siguiente me llamaron, me dijeron que el dinero lo dejara en la esquina de la "Cancha de los Olivos," (que es un lote abandonado), que si seguía los órdenes todo iba a estar bien. Con mucho miedo lleve el dinero y no supe nada mas.

6. A los 6 meses llegaron dos sujetos armados a mi casa, me dijeron por tu trabajo tienes que entregarnos una cantidad de $25 dolares semanales, es una orden. Me dijeron que si no pagaba, se iban a cobrar con mi vida.

7. Con mucho esfuerzo estuve pagando esta cantidad por muchos años. Ellos iban a recoger este dinero todo los sabados a cualquier hora a mi casa, ellos tocaban en la puerta y yo les entregaba el dinero. Cada sabado yo me quedaba en casa esperandolos. Eran diferentes personas que iban a recoger este dinero que siempre se les daba en efectivo. Yo estuve pagando este dinero desde el 2011 hasta Enero del 2015, cuando ya nos decidimos ir de el país.

8. El dia 20 de Diciembre del 2014 otra vez llegaron unos sujetos armados a mi casa cubiertos de sus rostros y vestidos similar a los de la policía de mi país. Empujaron la puerta y se metieron por la fuerza y me dijeron que iban a cambiar las leyes de la colonia. Que ya no iban a ser $25 dolares sino $500 dolares mensuales. Estás persona me dijeron que como yo era empleado de ANDA, y tenía un salario muy bueno de $695 dolares mensuales, tendria que pagar esta cantidad y que la

tenía que pagar inmediatamente. Estas personas me amenazaron con violar a mi esposa y hija, en persona cuando fueron a recoger el dinero. En esos momentos yo solo tenia $300 dolares, y ellos me dijeron prepárate con el resto del dinero si no ya sabes que le va a pasar a tu mujer y hija. Las vamos a violar y matar enfrente de ti. También me dijeron que si no seguía pagando me iban a matar a mi, y que nuestras vidas dependían del dinero que yo les tenía que pagar. Me volvieron a amenazar, me dijeron que no me fuera a mover, porque donde quiera que me fuera me iban a encontrar y me iban a torturar. Ellos también me dijeron que iban hacer los mismo que le hicieron a las Valladares (las cuñadas de mi hermano que fueron, secuestrada, violadas y luego las encontraron en un cementerio clandestino después de seis meses).

9. El 31 de Diciembre, veníamos de la iglesia mis hijos caminaban como a 200 pies de distancia mía y de lo oscuro salieron 4 sujetos. Uno de ellos agarró a mi hija, mi hija me gritó. Yo corrí a darle auxilio. Entonces me agarraron los 3 sujetos me comenzaron a golpear, yo me quise defender, pero no pude me votaron. Yo caí en la cuneta me pegaban a patadas, y con las manos el sujeto que tenía a mi hija la soltó. Ellos con la pistola en mano me amenazaban y me golpeaban. Con la pistola un hombre me pego en mi frente no supe quien era por que tenían sus rostros cubiertos, me decían que ahora si me iban a matar. Mi esposa y hijo les pedían que no me mataran. Después me dejaron creo que por los ruegos de mi familia, pero me dijeron que esto había sido solo una advertencia. Me dijeron que si no les seguía pagando, si los denunciaba o que si me movía de lugar, a mi hija y esposa las iban a violar y luego a matar. Me dijeron que me recordara lo que le paso a las cuñadas de mi hermano y que lo mismo nos iba a pasar a nosotros.

10. Esa noche decidimos irnos a otro cuidad llamada Sonsonate, que está a tres horas de donde vivíamos, y nos quedamos con mi padre, porque tuvimos miedo de que regresaran a matarnos. Mi hija estaba llorando y me dijo que el sujeto que la agarro le toco sus pechos y que le trato de tocar sus partes íntimas. Mi hija tenía y sigue teniendo miedo de que la vayan a violar. Por temor tuvimos que dejar todo lo que teníamos en la casa.

11. El 19 de Enero del 2015, mi esposa recibió otra llamada, le decian que ya tenian autorizacion para matarnos. Le dijeron que como no habíamos entregado el dinero y como nos movimos "les vamos a quebrar el culo." También le dijeron que ya estaban avisando a todos sus contactos. Nos mandaron un mensaje de texto donde me decían que si salia mi mujer le iban a destrozar su ano, y le iban a dejar su pecho perforado de puros balazos. Porque de ellos nadie se burlaba, ni se escaparon. También dijeron que nos iban a encontrar donde quiera que nos fuéramos y nos iban a matar. Por eso no tuvimos otra opción y abandonar nuestro pais.

12. Nunca reportamos nada de esto por el mismo temor de que nos fueran a matar no solo a nosotros, sino tambien a nuestros padres. También por que estas personas tienen a personas dentro del sistema policiaco, como ellos me dijeron las varias veces que me amenazaron.

13. Desde que nos fuimos, lo último que me entere es que estas personas se metieron a robar todo lo que estaba en mi casa. Quiero aclarar que ellos son categorizados como "Terroristas," son diferentes a las "Maras."

14. Por esta razones son las que no solo yo pero mi esposa e hijos tememos de regresar a nuestro país. Si nosotros llegáramos ir a El Salvador, por seguro nos matan porque estas personas piensan que nos burlamos de ellos, nosotros tenemos mucho temor de regresar.

Declaro bajo pena de perjurio bajo las leyes del Estado de California que lo anterior es verdadero y correcto. Ejecutado en Long Beach, California .

Date: 03/14/16

Wuiliam Edgardo CALDERON-ESPINOZA

EXHIBIT '2':
Family Registry

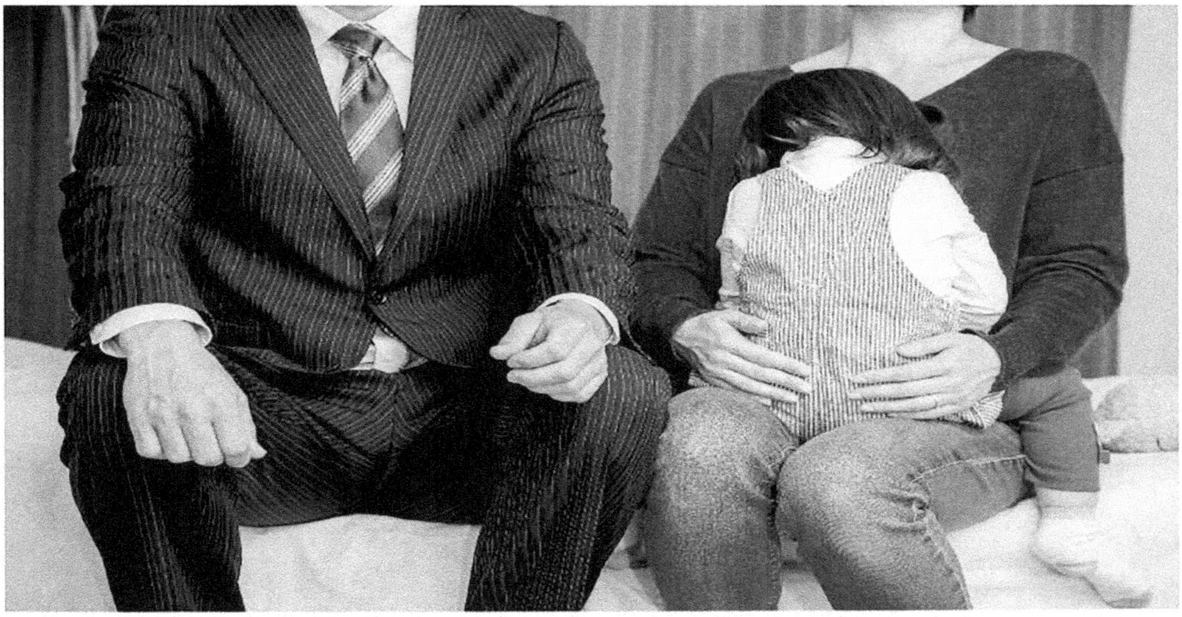

***** English Extract of Spanish Family Registry*****
Civil Registration

Name of the Bride:	Sandra Liseth Lopez Cierra
Name of the Groom:	Wilian Edgardo Calderon Espinoza
Date of Marriage:	02/09/ 2001

*****Certificate Information*****

Issue Date:	05/12/2015
Place of Issue:	Villa Santa Isabel Ishuatan, El Salvador
Magistrate:	Patricia Ermelinda De Leon Avalos
Record Location:	Villa Santa Isabel Ishuatan, El Salvador
Certificate No.: .	19

Translator's Certificate of Competence

I, Tanya Stewart, certify that the above is an accurate translation of the original Family Registry in Spanish and that I am competent in both English and Spanish to render such translation.

_____*Tanya Stewart*_____
Tanya Stewart

3 · 15 · 2016
Date

Law Offices of Brian D. Lerner
3233 East Broadway
Long Beach, CA 90803
Tel: (562) 495-0554

Alcaldía Municipal de Villa Santa Isabel Ishuatán
Departamento de Sonsonate, El Salvador, C.A.
Tel 2420-6400. Fax 2420-6408

EL SUSCRITO JEFE DEL REGISTRO FAMILIAR,

CERTIFICA: que a página CIENTO TREINTA Y SEIS del tomo UNO del Libro de Partidas de Nacimiento Número OCHENTA Y UNO que esta Oficina llevó en el año de mil novecientos ochenta , se encuentra asentada la que literalmente dice: Partida Número ciento cuatro -. SANDRA LISETH , hembra, nació a las nueve horas del día ocho de julio de mil novecientos ochenta , en el Cantón Acachapa de esta jurisdicción, siendo hija de RODELMY CIERRA , Oficios Domésticos, originaria de esta población, del domicilio de esta misma, de nacionalidad Salvadoreña.- Dio estos datos don JOSE NORBERTO LOPEZ de treinta años, agricultor, de este origen y domicilio, Salvadoreño, quien manifiesta ser Padre de la recién nacida, presentó Cédula de Identidad Personal número cero seis catorce quinientos ochenta, expedida por las Autoridades Municipales de esta población y firma juntamente con el Alcalde y Secretario. Oficina del Registro Civil que autoriza.- Alcaldía Municipal: Villa Santa Isabel Ishuatán, diecisiete de julio de mil novecientos ochenta .-.- R. Ant. Cortez/// J. Gonzalez ///J. P. Alvarado.///srio.- RUBRICADAS.- Número veintidos . Margínese la partida de nacimiento ciento cuatro del Libro de Partidas de Nacimiento que esta Oficina llevó en el año de mil novecientos ochenta en el sentido que la inscrita SANDRA LISETH LOPEZ CIERRA, contrajo matrimonio civil con WILIAN EDGARDO CALDERON ESPINOZA, según consta en el Acta Matrimonial número diecinueve acto celebrado ante los oficios del señor Alcalde Municipal, en la Alcaldia de Colón, el día nueve de febrero del presente año.- La Contrayente decide usar sus Apellidos de casada LOPEZ DE CALDERON.-. Alcaldía Municipal de Villa Santa Isabel Ishuatán, veintitres de febrero de dos mil uno ..- Alcalde;M. A.Gámez//Srio.;C. Campos de Espinoza//.- RUBRICADAS.- . Es conforme con su original con el cual se confrontó y para los efectos de Ley se expide la presente en la Oficina del Registro del Estado Familiar Alcaldía Municipal de Villa Santa Isabel Ishuatán el día doce de mayo de dos mil quince /////.- //

Patricia Ermelinda De Leon Avalos
Jefe del Registro del Estado Familiar

EXHIBIT '3':
Death Certificate

*** English Extract of Spanish Death Certificate***
Civil Registration

Name of Deceased:	Karen Alejandra Valladares
Sex:	Female
Date of Death:	03/15/2012
Place of Death:	Colon, El Salvador
Cause of Death:	Trauma to skull, facial and cervix with a knife.

Certificate Information

Issue Date:	04/20/2012
Place of Issue:	Colon, El Salvador
Medical Examiner:	Dr. Oscar Armando Quijano Aguilar
Record Location:	Colon, El Salvador
Certificate No.:	01689739-2

Translator's Certificate of Competence

I, Tanya Stewart, certify that the above is an accurate translation of the original Death Certificate in Spanish and that I am competent in both English and Spanish to render such translation.

_____Tanya Stewart_____ 3 · 15 · 2016
Tanya Stewart Date

Law Offices of Brian D. Lerner
3233 East Broadway
Long Beach, CA 90803
Tel: (562) 495-0554

INSTITUTO DE MEDICINA LEGAL
"DR. ROBERTO MASFERRER"

ESQUELA

HACE CONSTAR: Que en Colon, L.L.
a las doce horas y — minutos, del día quince
de Marzo del año dos mil doce se ha reconoci
cadáver de: Karen Alejandra Valladares Zolo
Dirección: Col. Granados, cton. Entierros, colon,

Quien según dictamen Médico Forense, adscrito al Instituto de Medicina L
"Dr. Roberto Masferrer", falleció a consecuencia de:
Trauma craneofacial y cervical con arma blanca

Se practica autopsia SÍ o NO. El cadáver se entrega a:
Francisca Adriana Valladares
DUI # 01689739-2

Y para los efectos de inhumación se extiende la presente
Santa Tecla, a las 13 hora
10 minutos del día 20
Abril del año dos mil doce.

F. [signature]
Dr. Oscar Armando Quijano Aguilar
Médico Forense
J.V.P.M. 4061

EXHIBIT '4':

Particular Social Group Statement

PARTICULAR SOCIAL GROUP STATEMENT

(1) Employees or Former Employees of Governmental Agencies

(2) Family: Members of the Calderon or Valladares Family

Translation from Spanish
3 July 2019

MUNICIPAL MAYOR'S OFFICE OF THE CITY OF COLON
FAMILY STATUS REGISTRY

BIRTH CERTIFICATE

INFORMATION ON REGISTRANT

1. REGISTRY OF BIRTHS OF THE MUNICIPALITY OF COLON
LA LIBERTAD PROVINCE
2. BOOK NUMBER: two, YEAR: two thousand and seven, FOLIO: five hundred and thirty-nine
3. CERTIFICATE NUMBER: five hundred and thirty-nine
4. REGISTRANT'S FIRST NAME: WILLIAN EDGARDO 5. SEX: male
6. BORN AT PRIMERO DE MAYO HOSPITAL
MUNICIPALITY OF SAN SALVADOR, SAN SALVADOR PROVINCE
7. AT EIGHT THIRTY-FIVE
ON June twenty-nine, two thousand and seven

INFORMATION ON THE MOTHER

8. SANDRA LISETH LOPEZ DE CALDERON
TWENTY-SEVEN YEARS OF AGE, OCCUPATION OR TRADE: HOUSEWIFE
9. BORN IN SANTA ISABEL ISHUATAN, SONSONATE
RESIDING IN COLON, LA LIBERTAD
10. NATIONALITY: SALVADORAN; 11. SHE IDENTIFIED HERSELF BY HER
unique identification document
NUMBER zero one four zero zero nine seven five - seven

INFORMATION ON THE FATHER

12. WUILIAM EDGARDO CALDERON ESPINOZA
TWENTY-EIGHT YEARS OF AGE, OCCUPATION OR TRADE: ELECTRICIAN
13. BORN IN APANECA, AHUACHAPAN
RESIDING IN COLON, LA LIBERTAD
14. NATIONALITY: SALVADORAN; 15. HE IDENTIFIED HIMSELF BY HIS
unique identification document
NUMBER zero one two eight five four eight four - seven

INFORMATION ON THE INFORMANT

16. THIS INFORMATION WAS PROVIDED BY
WUILIAM EDGARDO CALDERON ESPINOZA
17. WHO IDENTIFIED HIMSELF BY HIS unique identification document
NUMBER zero one two eight five four eight four - seven
18. HE DECLARED THAT HE WAS THE FATHER
AND SIGNED FOR THE RECORD, OR IF NOT - - - - - DOING SO,
LEFT HIS FINGERPRINT OF THE - - - - - [finger] OF HIS - - - - - HAND.
19. RECORDED BY VIRTUE OF - - - - -
DATED - - - - - OF - - - - - .

INFORMATION ON THE WITNESSES

20. WITH THE DECLARATIONS OF THE WITNESSES OF - - - - -
21. - - - - - - - - - - - - - - - -
WHO IDENTIFIED HIMSELF BY - - - - - NUMBER - - - - -
22. - - - - - - - - - - - - - - - - - - -
WHO IDENTIFIED HIMSELF BY - - - - - NUMBER - - - - -
23. PLACE AND DATE: COLON, July three, two thousand and seven
24. - - - - - -

25. [Signature] INFORMANT — WITNESS 1 — WITNESS 2 — [Signature] NAME AND SIGNATURE OF FAMILY STATUS REGISTRAR
Teresa Adelé Gonzalez de Ruiz

MARGIN NOTES

THE UNDERSIGNED CHIEF OF THE FAMILY STATUS REGISTRY OF THIS CITY CERTIFIES: That the original of this photocopy is recorded in the Book of Birth CERTIFICATES on page 539 for the year 2007 Volume 02.

This [copy] is being issued for any legal purposes by the Municipal Mayor's Office of the City of Colón.

JAN 09 2015 [Signature]
CHIEF, FAMILY STATUS REGISTRY

Rosetta Stone Translations, Tucson
Tel 520 575 9200 • rosettrans@aol.com • www.rosettrans.com

ALCALDIA MUNICIPAL DE CIUDAD COLON
REGISTRO DEL ESTADO FAMILIAR.

PARTIDA DE NACIMIENTO

DATOS DEL INSCRITO
1) REGISTRO DE NACIMIENTOS DEL MUNICIPIO DE COLON
DEPARTAMENTO DE LA LIBERTAD
2) LIBRO NÚMERO dos , AÑO dos mil siete , FOLIO quinientos treinta y nueve
3) PARTIDA NÚMERO quinientos treinta y nueve
4) NOMBRE PROPIO DEL INSCRITO WILLIAN EDGARDO 5)SEXO Masculino
6) NACIÓ EN HOSPITAL PRIMERO DE MAYO
MUNICIPIO DE SAN SALVADOR , DEPARTAMENTO DE SAN SALVADOR
7) A LAS ocho HORAS Y treinta y cinco MINUTOS,
DEL DÍA veintinueve DEL MES DE Junio DEL AÑO dos mil siete

DATOS DE LA MADRE
8) SANDRA LISETH LOPEZ DE CALDERON
DE veintiseis AÑOS DE EDAD, PROFESIÓN U OFICIO DEL HOGAR
9) ORIGINARIA DE SANTA ISABEL ISHUATAN , SONSONATE
DEL DOMICILIO DE COLON , LA LIBERTAD
10)DE NACIONALIDAD SALVADOREÑA 11)QUIEN SE IDENTIFICA POR MEDIO DE Documento Unico de Identidad
NÚMERO cero uno cuatro cero cero nueve siete cinco - siete

DATOS DEL PADRE
12)WUILIAM EDGARDO CALDERON ESPINOZA
DE veintiocho AÑOS DE EDAD, PROFESIÓN U OFICIO ELECTRICISTA
13)ORIGINARIO DE APANECA , AHUACHAPAN
DEL DOMICILIO DE COLON , LA LIBERTAD
14)DE NACIONALIDAD SALVADOREÑA 15)QUIEN SE IDENTIFICA POR MEDIO DE Documento Unico de Identidad
NÚMERO cero uno dos ocho cinco cuatro ocho cuatro - siete

DATOS DEL INFORMANTE
16)DIO ESTOS DATOS
WUILIAM EDGARDO CALDERON ESPINOZA
17)QUIEN SE IDENTIFICA POR MEDIO DE Documento Unico de Identidad
NÚMERO cero uno dos ocho cinco cuatro ocho cuatro - siete
18)MANIFESTANDO SER PADRE
Y PARA CONSTANCIA FIRMA O POR NO ----- HACERLO,
DEJA IMPRESA LA HUELLA DACTILAR DEL ----- DE SU MANO -----
19)SE ASIENTA EN VIRTUD DE -----
DE FECHA ----- DE ----- DE -----

DATOS DE LOS TESTIGOS
20)CON LAS DECLARACIONES DE LOS TESTIGOS DE -----
21)----- ----- -----
QUIEN SE IDENTIFICA POR MEDIO DE -----
NÚMERO -----
22)----- ----- -----
QUIEN SE IDENTIFICA POR MEDIO DE -----
NÚMERO -----
23)LUGAR Y FECHA: COLON , tres DE Julio DE dos mil siete
24)-----

25) INFORMANTE | TESTIGO 1 | TESTIGO 2 | NOMBRE Y FIRMA DEL REGISTRADOR DEL ESTADO FAMILIAR

Teresa Adela González de Ortiz

MARGINACIONES

... ESTADO FAMILIAR DE ... la fotocopia se encuentra ... 2007 ... 02 ... número ... folio 539 del ... Municipal de Ciudad Colón

19 ENE 2015

JEFA DEL REGISTRO DEL ESTADO FAMILIAR

EXHIBIT '5':
Respondent's Birth Certificate and Passport

296	Certificate No: One Hundred and Fifty: Wuiliam Edgardo Calderón Espinoza, male, was born at three-thirty in the morning on the eleventh day of this month in the Culiario Neighborhood of this village. [The child] is the son of Francisco Irene Calderón and of Marta Eroida Espinoza; the former being twenty-one years of age, a small-plot farmer, and the latter being twenty-one years of age, a housewife, both born in [illegible], Province of Sonsonate and residing here [illegible]. This information was provided by the newborn's father who identified himself by producing his Personal Identification Card number eleven-eight-zero zero zero four hundred and seventeen, issued in this office. He signed this certificate together with the undersigned Chief Civil Registrar who attests hereto. The undersigned certifying Chief Civil Registrar confirms that the informant identified himself in proper legal form. - The Civil Registry of the Municipal Mayor's Office, [illegible], on this eighteen day of June, nineteen hundred and seventy-nine. - Corrected = the = in order. Between the lines - / born here / = in order. - [illegible] deleted = eleven = farmer = in order. = [Signature] [Signature]

296

Partida Número Ciento Cincuenta: William Edgardo
Calderón Espinoza, Varón, Nació a las doce horas con
treinta Minutos del día Once del mes Corriente, en el Barrio El Calvario de esta Villa, siendo hijo de Francisco Jose Calderón, y de María Basilia Espinoza; el primero de Veintitres
años de edad, agricultor, [illegible] (de este origen) (el segundo), de Veintiuno
años de edad, de oficios domésticos, originarios de [illegible]
departamento de [illegible], [illegible] de este domicilio, hondu-
reños. Dió estos datos el padre del recién Nacido, quien exhibió
Cédula de identidad personal número once-ocho cero cero
cuatro cientos diecisiete, expedida en esta ciudad. Y firma la presente partida juntamente con el suscrito Jefe del Registro Civil y
[illegible]. El suscrito Jefe del Registro Civil que autoriza da
fé que el informante se identificó en legal forma. Registro Civil de la Alcaldía Municipal. [illegible], a los diecisiete días del
mes de Junio de mil novecientos setenta y nueve. Enmendado
= los = Vale. Entre líneas = de este origen = Vale. Sobre
borrado = once = agricultor = Vale.

[illegible signature] [illegible signature]

ROSETTA STONE _ASSOCIATES IN TRANSLATION_
7375 N. Calle sin Celo, Tucson, AZ 85718 • (520) 575-9200 • rosettrans@aol.com • www.rosettrans.com
• ATA-Certified •

Certification

AT THE REQUEST OF THE INTERESTED PARTY, I hereby certify that I have translated the following document:

Birth Certificate of Wuiliam Edgardo Calderón Espinoza

from the Spanish into the English language on this 3rd day of July 2019, and that the information contained in the translated document is a true, complete and correct reflection of the original text, to the best of my ability as a Professional Translator.

ROSETTA STONE ASSOCIATES IN TRANSLATION

Carola P. Myers

CAROLA P. MYERS
Member, A.C.I.A. - ATA-Accredited

Your Dependable Source of Foreign Language Translation and Interpretation

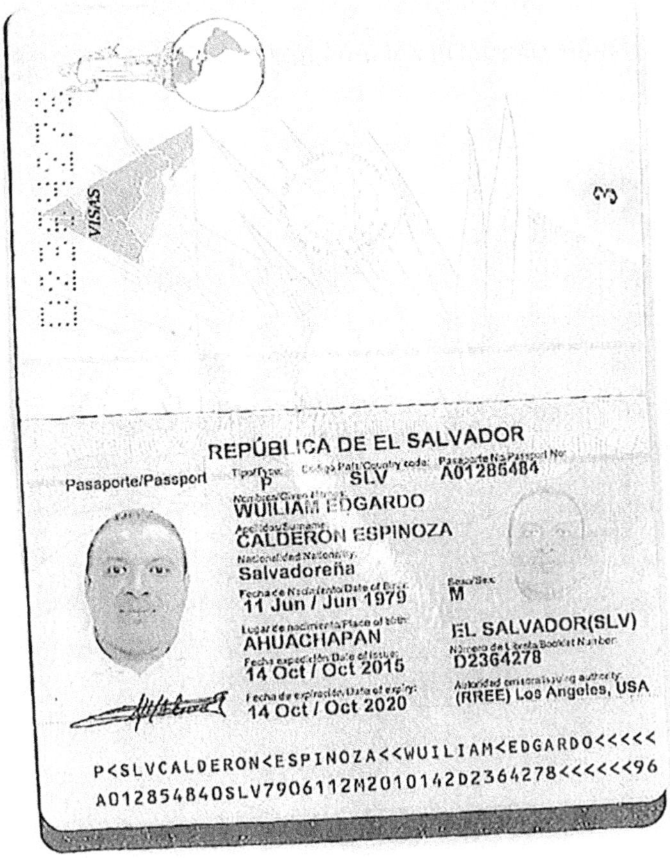
VISAS
REPÚBLICA DE EL SALVADOR
Pasaporte/Passport
P
SLV
A01285484
WUILIAM EDGARDO
CALDERON ESPINOZA
Salvadoreña
11 Jun / Jun 1979
M
AHUACHAPAN
EL SALVADOR(SLV)
14 Oct / Oct 2015
D2364278
14 Oct / Oct 2020
(RREE) Los Angeles, USA
P<SLVCALDERON<ESPINOZA<<WUILIAM<EDGARDO<<<<<
A012854840SLV7906112M2010142D2364278<<<<<<96

39

EXHIBIT '6':
Respondent's Marriage Certificate

Translation from Spanish
3 July 2019

MUNICIPAL MAYOR'S OFFICE OF COLON

PROVINCE OF LA LIBERTAD
EL SALVADOR, C.A.

FAMILY STATUS REGISTRY
MARRIAGE CERTIFICATE

Folio 21

Certificate Number twenty-one. Mr. WUILIAM EDGARDO CALDERON ESPINOZA and SANDRA LISETH LOPEZ CIERRA, the former twenty-one years of age, born in Apaneca, legal status single, occupation student residing in Apaneca nationality Salvadoran
son of Francisco Irene Calderón, farmer, residing in Sonsonate,
and of Marta Eroida Espinoza, housewife, residing in Sonsonate,
the latter being twenty years of age, born in Santa Isabel Ishuatán, legal status single, occupation employee, residing in Santa Isabel Ishuatán, nationality Salvadoran daughter of José Norberto López, employee, residing here
and of Rodelmy Cierra, deceased.

They were civilly married before Guillermo González Huezo, Municipal Mayor
on February nine of this year at two o'clock in the afternoon
in presence of the witnesses: Rafael de Jesús Delcón
and Douglas Antonio Hernández. Pursuant to Article 14 of the Law on Names of Natural Persons, the bride has chosen to use the following name: Sandra Liseth López de Calderón, and [the couple] have chosen the deferred community property regimen.
During the proceedings, they have recognized as their children: =====
who shall use the surnames of: =====
The Municipal Mayor's Office of Colón, this ninth day of February, two thousand and one.

[Signature]
In charge of the Family Status Registry
TERESA ADELI GONZALEZ DE RUIZ

THE UNDERSIGNED CHIEF OF THE FAMILY STATUS REGISTRY OF THIS CITY CERTIFIES: That the original of this photocopy is recorded in the Book of *Marriage* CERTIFICATES on page 21 for the year 2001 Volume 04.

This [copy] is being issued for any legal purposes by the Municipal Mayor's Office of the City of Colón.

SEP. 2, 2015 [Signature]
CHIEF, FAMILY STATUS REGISTRY
Teresa Adeli Gonzalez De Ruiz

Rosetta Stone Translations • Tucson, Arizona
(520) 575-9200 • rosettrans@aol.com • www.rosettrans.com

ALCALDIA MUNICIPAL DE COLON

DEPARTAMENTO DE LA LIBERTAD
EL SALVADOR, C.A.

REGISTRO DEL ESTADO FAMILIAR
PARTIDA DE MATRIMONIO

Folio 21

Partida Número veintiún. Los señores WUILIAM EDGARDO CALDERON ESPINOZA y SANDRA LISETH LOPEZ CIERRA, el primero de veintiún años de edad, originario de Apaneca, estado civil soltero, ocupación estudiante del domicilio de Apaneca, de nacionalidad Salvadoreña siendo hijo de Francisco Irene Calderón, agricultor, del domicilio de Sonsonate.

y de Marta Eroida Espinoza, de oficios domésticos, del domicilio de Sonsonate.

la segunda de veinte años de edad, originaria de Santa Isabel Ishuatán, estado civil soltera, ocupación empleada del domicilio de Santa Isabel Ishuatán, de nacionalidad Salvadoreña siendo hija de José Norberto López, empleado, de este domicilio

y de Rodelmy Cierra, ya fallecida.

Contrajeron Matrimonio Civil ante los oficios de Guillermo González Huezo Alcalde Municipal

a las catorce horas del día nueve de febrero del corriente año estando presente los testigos: Rafael de Jesus Deleón y Douglas Antonio Hernández, de conformidad al Art. 14 de la Ley del Nombre de la Persona Natural, la contrayente decide usar el nombre así ::: Sandra Liseth Lópes de Calderón y optan por el régimen patrimonial de Comunidad Diferida.

En el acto reconocen como hijo(s) a ====

quienes usarán los apellidos: ====.

Alcaldía Municipal de Colón, a nueve de febrero de dos mil uno.

Enc. Reg. Estado Familiar
[illegible]A ADELI GONZALEZ DE RUIZ.

EL INFRASCRITO (A) JEFE(A) DEL REGISTRO DEL ESTADO FAMILIAR DE ESTA CIUDAD, CERTIFICA: Que el archivo original de la presente fotocopia se encuentra asentado en el libro de PARTIDAS DE: Matrimonio a folio 21 del año 2001 tomo [illegible]

y para efectos legales [illegible]. Alcaldía Municipal de Ciudad Colón

0 2 SEP 2015

JEFE DEL REGISTRO DEL ESTADO [illegible]

ROSETTA STONE *ASSOCIATES IN TRANSLATION*
7375 N. Calle sin Celo, Tucson, AZ 85718 • (520) 575-9200 • rosettrans@aol.com • www.rosettrans.com
• ATA-Certified •

Certification

AT THE REQUEST OF THE INTERESTED PARTY, I hereby certify that I have translated the following document:

Marriage Certificate of Wuiliam Edgardo Calderón E.
and Sandra Liseth Lopez C.

from the Spanish into the English language on this 3rd day of July 2019, and that the information contained in the translated document is a true, complete and correct reflection of the original text, to the best of my ability as a Professional Translator.

ROSETTA STONE ASSOCIATES IN TRANSLATION

Carola P. Myers

CAROLA P. MYERS
Member, A.C.I.A. - ATA-Accredited

Your Dependable Source of Foreign Language Translation and Interpretation

EXHIBIT '7':
Respondent's Spouse Birth Certificate and Passport

Translation from Spanish
3 July 2019

Municipal Mayor's Office of Villa Santa Isabel Ishuatán
Province of Sonsonate, El Salvador, C.A.
Tel. 2420-6400. Fax 2420-6408

THE UNDERSIGNED CHIEF OF THE FAMILY REGISTRY

CERTIFIES: That on page ONE HUNDRED AND THIRTY-SIX of Volume ONE of the Book of Birth Certificates Number EIGHTY-ONE which was maintained by this Office in the year nineteen hundred and eighty, there appears an entry which reads verbatim: Certificate Number one hundred and four. - SANDRA LISETH, female, was born at nine o'clock in the morning on July eight, nineteen hundred and eighty in the Canton of Acachapa in this jurisdiction. She is the daughter of RODELMY CIERRA, a housewife, a Salvadoran national, born in this village and also residing here. - This information was provided by Mr. JOSE NORBERTO LOPEZ, thirty years of age, a farmer, a Salvadoran national, born and residing here, who declares that he is the father of the newborn. He presented his Personal Identification Card number zero six fourteen five hundred and eighty, issued by the Municipal Authorities of this village. He signed [this certificate] together with the Mayor and Secretary. The certifying Civil Registry. - Municipal Mayor's Office: Villa Santa Isabel Ishuatán, July seventeen, nineteen hundred and eighty. -.- R. Ant. Cortez. /// J. Gonzalez /// J. P. Alvarado. /// Secretary. - FLOURISHES. - Number twenty-two. An annotation shall be made in the margin of birth certificate one hundred and four of the Book of Birth Certificates maintained by this Office in the year nineteen hundred and eighty to the effect that the registrant SANDRA LISETH LOPEZ CIERRA was civilly married to WILIAN EDGARDO CALDERON ESPINOZA, as reflected in the Marriage Certificate number nineteen. The marriage was entered into before the Municipal Mayor at the Mayor's Office at Colón on February nine of this year. - The bride has decided to use her married last names of LOPEZ DE CALDERON. - Municipal Mayor's Office, Village of Santa Isabel Ishuatán, February twenty-three, two thousand and one. - The Mayor: A. Gámez // Secretary: C. Campos de Espinoza // - FLOURISHES. - This [copy] agrees with the original with which it was compared. This certificate is being issued for any legal purposes in the Office of the Legal Status Registry, Mayor's Office of Villa Santa Isabel Ishuatán on this twelfth day of May, two thousand and fifteen. ////

[*Signature*]
Patricia Ermelinda De Leon Avalos
Chief, Family Status Registry

MUNICIPAL MAYOR'S OFFICE SANTA ISABEL ISHUATÁN FAMILY STATUS REGISTRY SONSONATE EL SALVADOR C.A.

Rosetta Stone Translations, Tucson
Tel. 520 575 9200 • rosettrans@aol.com • www.rosettrans.com

Alcaldía Municipal de Villa Santa Isabel Ishuatán
Departamento de Sonsonate, El Salvador, C.A.
Tel 2420-6400. Fax 2420-6408

EL SUSCRITO JEFE DEL REGISTRO FAMILIAR,

CERTIFICA: que a página CIENTO TREINTA Y SEIS del tomo UNO del Libro de Partidas de Nacimiento Número OCHENTA Y UNO que esta Oficina llevó en el año de mil novecientos ochenta , se encuentra asentada la que literalmente dice: Partida Número ciento cuatro -. SANDRA LISETH , hembra, nació a las nueve horas del día ocho de julio de mil novecientos ochenta , en el Cantón Acachapa de esta jurisdicción, siendo hija de RODELMY CIERRA , Oficios Domésticos, originaria de esta población, del domicilio de esta misma, de nacionalidad Salvadoreña.- Dio estos datos don JOSE NORBERTO LOPEZ de treinta años, agricultor, de este origen y domicilio, Salvadoreño, quien manifiesta ser Padre de la recién nacida, presentó Cédula de Identidad Personal número cero seis catorce quinientos ochenta, expedida por las Autoridades Municipales de esta población y firma juntamente con el Alcalde y Secretario. Oficina del Registro Civil que autoriza.- Alcaldía Municipal: Villa Santa Isabel Ishuatán, diecisiete de julio de mil novecientos ochenta .-.- R. Ant. Cortez/// J. Gonzalez ///J. P. Alvarado.///srio.- RUBRICADAS.- Número veintidos . Margínese la partida de nacimiento ciento cuatro del Libro de Partidas de Nacimiento que esta Oficina llevó en el año de mil novecientos ochenta en el sentido que la inscrita SANDRA LISETH LOPEZ CIERRA, contrajo matrimonio civil con WILIAN EDGARDO CALDERON ESPINOZA, según consta en el Acta Matrimonial número diecinueve acto celebrado ante los oficios del señor Alcalde Municipal, en la Alcaldia de Colón, el día nueve de febrero del presente año.- La Contrayente decide usar sus Apellidos de casada LOPEZ DE CALDERON.-. Alcaldía Municipal de Villa Santa Isabel Ishuatán, veintitres de febrero de dos mil uno ..- Alcalde;M. A.Gámez//Srio.;C. Campos de Espinoza//.- RUBRICADAS.- . Es conforme con su original con el cual se confrontó y para los efectos de Ley se expide la presente en la Oficina del Registro del Estado Familiar Alcaldía Municipal de Villa Santa Isabel Ishuatán el día doce de mayo de dos mil quince /////.- //

Patricia Ermelinda De León Avalos
Jefe del Registro del Estado Familiar

ROSETTA STONE *ASSOCIATES IN TRANSLATION*
7375 N. Calle sin Celo, Tucson, AZ 85718 • (520) 575-9200 • rosettrans@aol.com • www.rosettrans.com
• ATA-Certified •

Certification

AT THE REQUEST OF THE INTERESTED PARTY, I hereby certify that I have translated the following document:

Birth Certificate of Sandra Liseth López Cierra

from the Spanish into the English language on this 3rd day of July 2019, and that the information contained in the translated document is a true, complete and correct reflection of the original text, to the best of my ability as a Professional Translator.

ROSETTA STONE ASSOCIATES IN TRANSLATION

Carola P. Myers

CAROLA P. MYERS
Member, A.C.I.A. - ATA-Accredited

Your Dependable Source of Foreign Language Translation and Interpretation

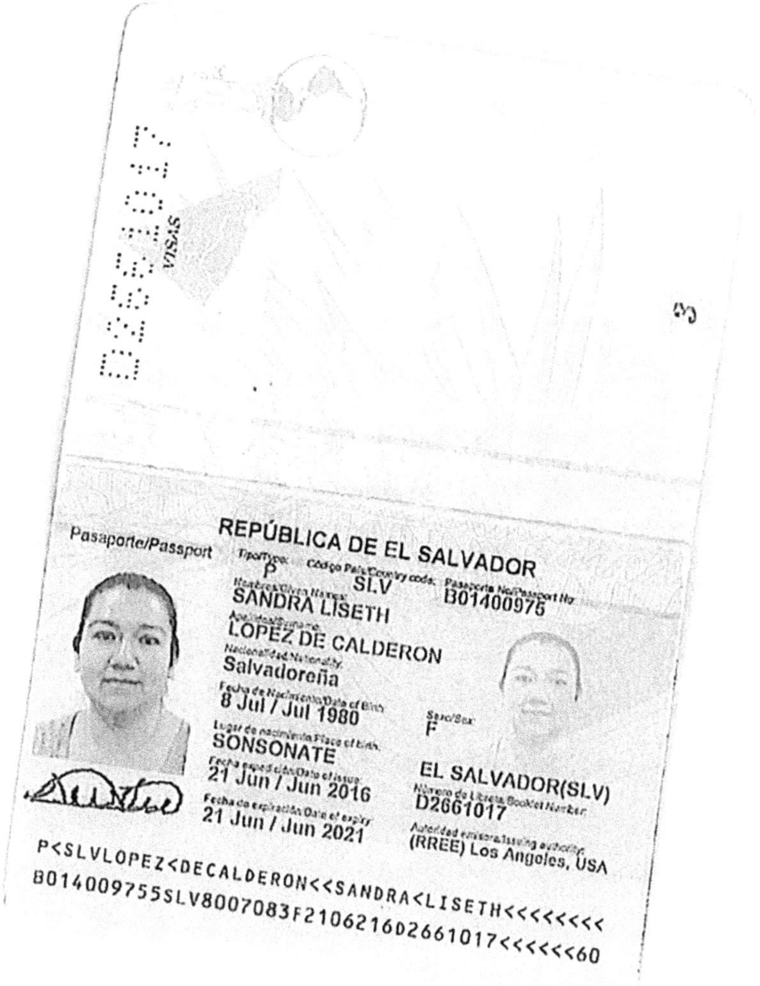
D2661017
VISAS
Pasaporte/Passport
REPÚBLICA DE EL SALVADOR
P
SLV
B01400975
SANDRA LISETH
LOPEZ DE CALDERON
Salvadoreña
8 Jul / Jul 1980
F
SONSONATE
EL SALVADOR(SLV)
21 Jun / Jun 2016
D2661017
21 Jun / Jun 2021
(RREE) Los Angeles, USA
P<SLVLOPEZ<DECALDERON<<SANDRA<LISETH<<<<<<<<<
B014009755SLV8007083F2106216D2661017<<<<<<60

EXHIBIT '8':
Respondent's Daughter Birth Certificate and Passport

Translation from Spanish
3 July 2019

Municipal Mayor's Office of Villa Santa Isabel Ishuatán
Province of Sonsonate, El Salvador, C.A.
Tel. 2420-6400. Fax 2420-6408

THE UNDERSIGNED CHIEF OF THE FAMILY REGISTRY

CERTIFIES: That on page NINETY-EIGHT of Volume ONE of the Book of Birth Certificates Number ONE HUNDRED AND TWO which was maintained by this Office in the year two thousand and one, there appears an entry which reads verbatim: Certificate Number one hundred and fifty. - KATHERINE RODELMY, female, was born at three fifteen in the morning on April twenty-four, two thousand and one in the National Hospital of Sonsonate. She is the daughter of WUILIAM EDGARDO CALDERON ESPINOZA, twenty-two years of age, a student, a Salvadoran national, born in Apaneca and residing here, and of SANDRA LISETH LOPEZ CIERRA, twenty years of age, an employee, a Salvadoran national, born in this village and residing here. - This information was provided by MARTA EROIDA ESPINOZA who declared that she was the grandmother of the newborn and presented her Personal Identification Card number zero six zero six zero zero zero nine thousand two hundred and seven. She signed [this certificate] together with the Mayor and Secretary. - The certifying Civil Registry. - Municipal Mayor's Office: Villa Santa Isabel Ishuatán, June twenty-nine, two thousand and one.-.- M. A. Gamez. /// Marta Eroila Espinoza. /// C. Campos E. /// Secretary. - FLOURISHES. - The informant paid the fine pursuant to Article 16 of the Incidental Law of the Family Status Registry. - This [copy] agrees with the original with which it was compared. This certificate is being issued for any legal purposes in the Office of the Legal Status Registry, Mayor's Office of Villa Santa Isabel Ishuatán on this thirteenth day of January, two thousand and fifteen. ////

[*Signature*]
Gustavo Adolfo Peña Valle
Chief, Family Status Registry

Alcaldía Municipal de Villa Santa Isabel Ishuatán
Departamento de Sonsonate, El Salvador, C.A.
Tel 2420-6400. Fax 2420-6408

LA SUSCRITA JEFE DEL REGISTRO FAMILIAR,

CERTIFICA: que a página NOVENTA Y OCHO del tomo UNO del Libro de Partidas de Nacimiento Número CIENTO DOS que esta Oficina llevó en el año de dos mil uno , se encuentra asentada la que literalmente dice: Partida Número ciento cincuenta -. KATHERINE RODELMY , hembra, nació a las tres horas quince minutos del dia veinticuatro de abril de dos mil uno , en el Hospital Nacional de Sonsonate, siendo hija de WUILIAM EDGARDO CALDERON ESPINOZA, de veintidos años de edad , Estudiante, originario de Apaneca, de este domicilio, de nacionalidad Salvadoreña y de SANDRA LISETH LOPEZ CIERRA, de veinte años de edad , Empleada, originaria de esta población, de este domicilio, de nacionalidad Salvadoreña.- Dio estos datos MARTA EROIDA ESPINOZA, quien manifiesta ser Abuela de la recién nacida, presentó Cédula de Identidad Personal número cero seis cero seis cero cero cero nueve mil doscientos siete y firma juntamente con el Alcalde y Secretario. Oficina del Registro Civil que autoriza.- Alcaldía Municipal: Villa Santa Isabel Ishuatán, veintinueve de junio de dos mil uno .-.- M. A. Gamez/// Marta Eroila Espinoza ///C. Campos E.///Sria.-.- RUBRICADAS.- La informante canceló multa conforme articulo 16 de la Ley Transitoria del Registro del Estado Familiar.- , Es conforme con su original con el cual se confrontó y para los efectos de Ley se expide la presente en la Oficina del Registro del Estado Familiar Alcaldía Municipal de Villa Santa Isabel Ishuatán el día trece de enero de dos mil quince /////.- ///

Gustavo Adolfo Peña Valle
Jefe del Registro del Estado Familiar

ROSETTA STONE *ASSOCIATES IN TRANSLATION*
7375 N. Calle sin Celo, Tucson, AZ 85718 • (520) 575-9200 • rosettrans@aol.com • www.rosettrans.com
• ATA-Certified •

Certification

AT THE REQUEST OF THE INTERESTED PARTY, I hereby certify that I have translated the following document:

Birth Certificate of Katherine Rodelmy Calderón López

from the Spanish into the English language on this 3rd day of July 2019, and that the information contained in the translated document is a true, complete and correct reflection of the original text, to the best of my ability as a Professional Translator.

ROSETTA STONE ASSOCIATES IN TRANSLATION

Carola P. Myers

CAROLA P. MYERS
Member, A.C.I.A. - ATA-Accredited

Your Dependable Source of Foreign Language Translation and Interpretation

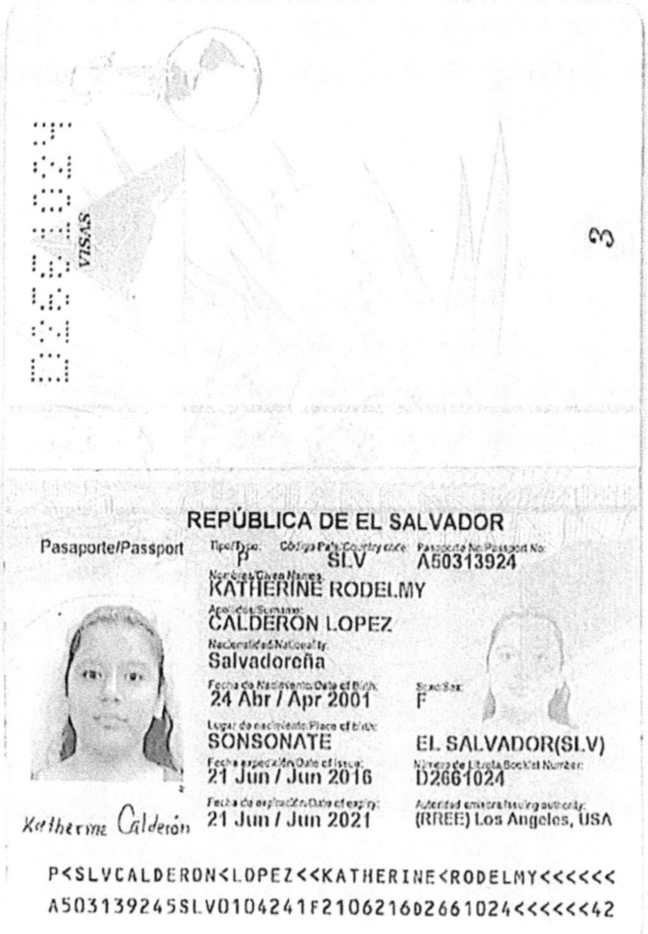

VISAS

3

REPÚBLICA DE EL SALVADOR

Pasaporte/Passport

Tipo/Type: P
Código País/Country code: SLV
Pasaporte No/Passport No: A50313924

Nombres/Given Names: KATHERINE RODELMY

Apellidos/Surname: CALDERON LOPEZ

Nacionalidad/Nationality: Salvadoreña

Fecha de Nacimiento/Date of Birth: 24 Abr / Apr 2001
Sexo/Sex: F

Lugar de nacimiento/Place of birth: SONSONATE
EL SALVADOR(SLV)

Fecha expedición/Date of issue: 21 Jun / Jun 2016
Número de Libreta/Booklet Number: D2661024

Fecha de expiración/Date of expiry: 21 Jun / Jun 2021
Autoridad emisora/Issuing authority: (RREE) Los Angeles, USA

Katherine Calderón

P<SLVCALDERON<LOPEZ<<KATHERINE<RODELMY<<<<<<

A503139245SLV0104241F2106216D2661024<<<<<<42

EXHIBIT '9':
Respondent's Son Birth Certificate and Passport

ROSETTA STONE *ASSOCIATES IN TRANSLATION*
7375 N. Calle sin Celo, Tucson, AZ 85718 • (520) 575-9200 • rosettrans@aol.com • www.rosettrans.com
• ATA-Certified •

Certification

AT THE REQUEST OF THE INTERESTED PARTY, I hereby certify that I have translated the following document:

Birth Certificate of Willian Edgardo Calderón Jr.

from the Spanish into the English language on this 3rd day of July 2019, and that the information contained in the translated document is a true, complete and correct reflection of the original text, to the best of my ability as a Professional Translator.

ROSETTA STONE ASSOCIATES IN TRANSLATION

Carola P. Myers

CAROLA P. MYERS
Member, A.C.I.A. - ATA-Accredited

Your Dependable Source of Foreign Language Translation and Interpretation

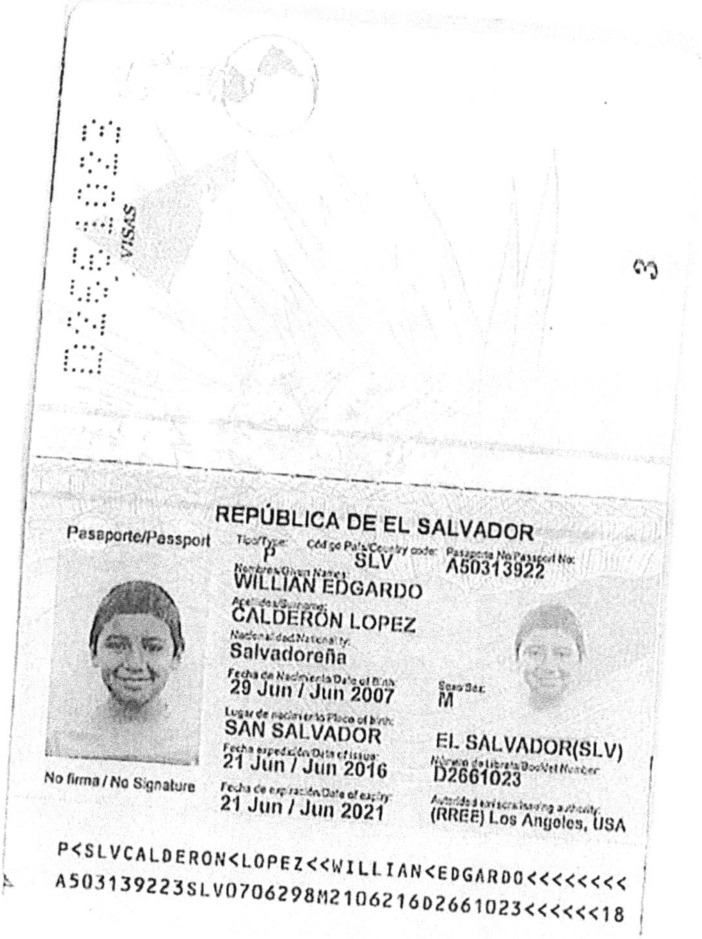

D2661023

VISAS

3

REPÚBLICA DE EL SALVADOR

Pasaporte/Passport

Tipo/Type: P

Código País/Country code: SLV

Pasaporte No/Passport No: A50313922

Nombres/Given Names: WILLIAN EDGARDO

Apellidos/Surname: CALDERON LOPEZ

Nacionalidad/Nationality: Salvadoreña

Fecha de Nacimiento/Date of Birth: 29 Jun / Jun 2007

Sexo/Sex: M

Lugar de nacimiento/Place of birth: SAN SALVADOR

EL SALVADOR(SLV)

Fecha expedición/Date of issue: 21 Jun / Jun 2016

Número de libreta/Booklet Number: D2661023

No firma / No Signature

Fecha de expiración/Date of expiry: 21 Jun / Jun 2021

Autoridad emisora/Issuing authority: (RREE) Los Angeles, USA

P<SLVCALDERON<LOPEZ<<WILLIAN<EDGARDO<<<<<<<<<

A503139223SLV0706298M2106216D2661023<<<<<<18

EXHIBIT '10':
Respondent's Criminal History Information (CALDOJ)

XAVIER BECERRA
Attorney General

State of California
DEPARTMENT OF JUSTICE

BUREAU OF CRIMINAL INFORMATION AND ANALYSIS
P.O. Box 903417
SACRAMENTO, CA 94203-4170

March 04, 2019

WUILIAM E CALDERONESPINOZA
130 E 81ST STREET
LOS ANGELES, CA 90003

RE: California Criminal History Information

Dear Applicant:

This is in response to your inquiry concerning the existence of a California criminal history record within the files of the Department of Justice's Bureau of Criminal Information and Analysis. As of the date of this letter, a search of your fingerprints did not identify with any criminal history record maintained by this Bureau as provided by the California Penal Code Sections 11120-11127. As requested, a copy of this record review has been sent to your designee.

Pursuant to California Penal Code section 11121, the purpose of a record review request is to afford an individual with a copy of their record and to refute any erroneous or inaccurate information contained therein. The intent is not to be used for licensing, certification or employment purposes.

Additionally, California Penal Code sections 11125, 11142, and 11143 does not allow for a person or agency to make a request to another person to provide them with a copy of an individual's criminal history or notification that a record does not exist; does not allow an authorized person to furnish the record to an unauthorized person; nor does it allow an unauthorized person to buy, receive or possess the record or information. A violation of these section codes is a misdemeanor.

Record Review and Challenge Program
Applicant Record and Certification Branch
Bureau of Criminal Information and Analysis

For XAVIER BECERRA
Attorney General

BCIA 8708d (Rev. 02/17)

EXHIBIT '11':
Respondent's Spouse Criminal History Information (CALDOJ)

XAVIER BECERRA
Attorney General

State of California
DEPARTMENT OF JUSTICE

BUREAU OF CRIMINAL INFORMATION AND ANALYSIS
P.O. Box 903417
SACRAMENTO, CA 94203-4170

March 04, 2019

SANDRA L LOPEZDECALDERON
130 E 81ST STREET
LOS ANGELES, CA 90003

RE: California Criminal History Information

Dear Applicant:

This is in response to your inquiry concerning the existence of a California criminal history record within the files of the Department of Justice's Bureau of Criminal Information and Analysis. As of the date of this letter, a search of your fingerprints did not identify with any criminal history record maintained by this Bureau as provided by the California Penal Code Sections 11120-11127. As requested, a copy of this record review has been sent to your designee.

Pursuant to California Penal Code section 11121, the purpose of a record review request is to afford an individual with a copy of their record and to refute any erroneous or inaccurate information contained therein. The intent is not to be used for licensing, certification or employment purposes.

Additionally, California Penal Code sections 11125, 11142, and 11143 does not allow for a person or agency to make a request to another person to provide them with a copy of an individual's criminal history or notification that a record does not exist; does not allow an authorized person to furnish the record to an unauthorized person; nor does it allow an unauthorized person to buy, receive or possess the record or information. A violation of these section codes is a misdemeanor.

Record Review and Challenge Program
Applicant Record and Certification Branch
Bureau of Criminal Information and Analysis

For XAVIER BECERRA
Attorney General

BCIA 8708d (Rev. 02/17)

EXHIBIT '12':
Respondent's Daughter Criminal History Information (CALDOJ)

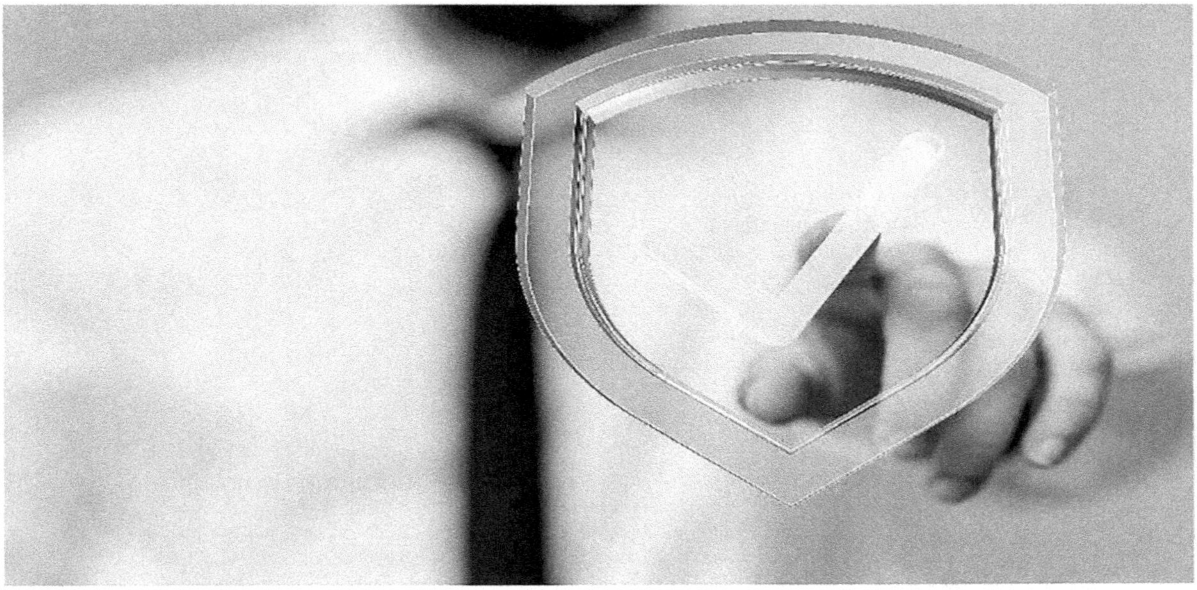

XAVIER BECERRA
Attorney General

State of California
DEPARTMENT OF JUSTICE

BUREAU OF CRIMINAL INFORMATION AND ANALYSIS
P.O. Box 903417
SACRAMENTO, CA 94203-4170

March 04, 2019

KATHERINE R CALDERON LOPEZ
130 E 81ST STREET
LOS ANGELES, CA 90003

RE: California Criminal History Information

Dear Applicant:

This is in response to your inquiry concerning the existence of a California criminal history record within the files of the Department of Justice's Bureau of Criminal Information and Analysis. As of the date of this letter, a search of your fingerprints did not identify with any criminal history record maintained by this Bureau as provided by the California Penal Code Sections 11120-11127. As requested, a copy of this record review has been sent to your designee.

Pursuant to California Penal Code section 11121, the purpose of a record review request is to afford an individual with a copy of their record and to refute any erroneous or inaccurate information contained therein. The intent is not to be used for licensing, certification or employment purposes.

Additionally, California Penal Code sections 11125, 11142, and 11143 does not allow for a person or agency to make a request to another person to provide them with a copy of an individual's criminal history or notification that a record does not exist; does not allow an authorized person to furnish the record to an unauthorized person; nor does it allow an unauthorized person to buy, receive or possess the record or information. A violation of these section codes is a misdemeanor.

Record Review and Challenge Program
Applicant Record and Certification Branch
Bureau of Criminal Information and Analysis

For XAVIER BECERRA
Attorney General

BCIA 8708d (Rev. 02/17)

EXHIBIT '13':

Letter of Former Employment for Respondent

Translation from Spanish
3 July 2019

THE UNDERSIGNED DIRECTOR OF HUMAN RESOURCES OF THE NATIONAL ADMINISTRATION OF AQUEDUCTS AND SEWER SYSTEMS, ANDA,

CERTIFIES:

That Mr. **Wuiliam Edgardo Calderón Espinoza** worked for this Institution from January fourteen, two thousand and two to March eleven, two thousand and fifteen, performing work as an **Electrician** at the Electromechanical Maintenance Management, Central Region; he worked under the **Daily Wage** system and earned a daily wage of $23.27 U.S. dollars.

I have issued, signed and sealed this Certificate in the city of San Salvador on this eighteenth day of March, two thousand and nineteen for presentation to the **Embassy of the United States of America**.

[*Signature*]
Jorge Alberto Bolaños Escudero, Esq.
Human Resources Director

HUMAN RESOURCES ANDA ADMINISTRATION

Rosetta Stone Translations, Tucson
Tel 520 575 9200 • rosettrans@aol.com • www.rosettrans.com

EL INFRASCRITO DIRECTOR DE RECURSOS HUMANOS DE LA ADMINISTRACION NACIONAL DE ACUEDUCTOS Y ALCANTARILLADOS, ANDA.

<u>HACE CONSTAR:</u>

Que el señor **Wulliam Edgardo Calderón Espinoza,** laboró en esta Institución desde el catorce de enero del dos mil dos al once de marzo del dos mil quince, desempeñando el cargo de **Electricista** en la Gerencia de Mantenimiento Electromecánico Región Central; nombrado bajo el sistema de **Jornal Diario,** devengando un salario diario de **$23.27** dólares de los Estados Unidos de América

Y para efectos de ser presentada en la **Embajada de los Estados Unidos de América,** extiendo firmo y sello la presente Constancia, en la ciudad de San Salvador, a los dieciocho días del mes de marzo del año dos mil diecinueve.

Lic. Jorge Alberto Bolaños Escudero
Director de Recursos Humanos

Dirección de Recursos Humanos
Colonia Libertad, Avenida Don Bosco, Edificio Ex IVU
San Salvador, El Salvador, C.A.

ROSETTA STONE *ASSOCIATES IN TRANSLATION*
7375 N. Calle sin Celo, Tucson, AZ 85718 • (520) 575-9200 • rosettrans@aol.com • www.rosettrans.com
• ATA-Certified •

Certification

AT THE REQUEST OF THE INTERESTED PARTY, I hereby certify that I have translated the following document:

Employment letter related to Wuiliam Edgardo Calderón Espinoza
dated March 18, 2019

from the Spanish into the English language on this 3rd day of July 2019, and that the information contained in the translated document is a true, complete and correct reflection of the original text, to the best of my ability as a Professional Translator.

ROSETTA STONE ASSOCIATES IN TRANSLATION

Carola P. Myers

CAROLA P. MYERS
Member, A.C.I.A. - ATA-Accredited

Your Dependable Source of Foreign Language Translation and Interpretation

EXHIBIT '14':
Letter from the Calderon Valladares Family

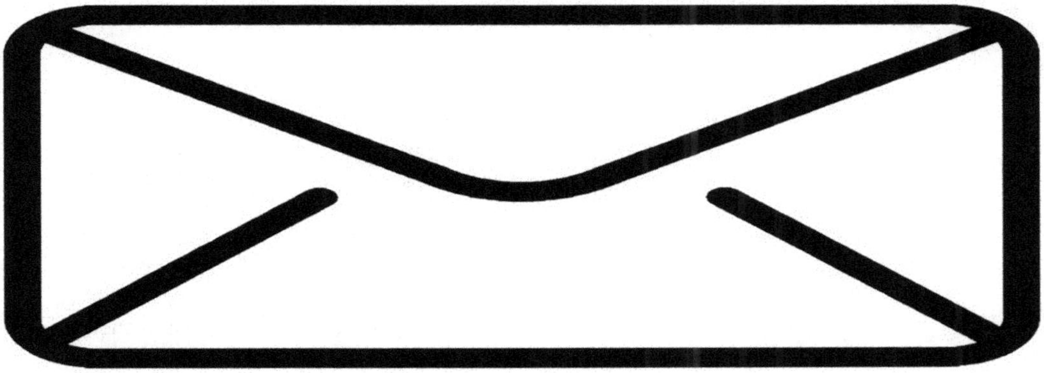

Translation from Spanish
3 July 2019

April 20, 2018

El Salvador, San Salvador.

To whom it may concern.

By means of this letter we, the Calderón Valladares family, certify to the traumatic episodes which we had to face with the disappearance and murder of our sisters Karen and Leslie Valladares and being witnesses to the threats made against my brother Wuiliam Calderón and his family we want to express our fear because they cannot return to our country because they may be killed by the terrorist groups who hide behind gang names [and] who are individuals without scruples or values they harassed him and his family because of the fact that he was working at a government agency, they subjected him to threats and constant monetary extortion, we were witnesses to the act of violence against him [and] his family, in which for helping his daughter against an individual who held her and touched her so that she was crying [and] told of the abuses he had committed, her father trying to help her was intercepted by another three subjects who awaited him hidden in the darkness barring his way to his daughter who was yelling for help. The subjects knocked him to the ground and kicked him and immobilized him, and one of them who carried a firearm touched him with it in front accusing him of giving information to some i9 [sic] investigators who had entered their residential area and captured members belonging to their outfit, they threatened to kill him telling him that he and his family were going to die at their hands on orders of their superiors and that if he reported them it wouldn't do any good because they had infiltrated the police, these were traumatic incidents for the Calderón family, and that's why we are expressing our fear and give our word that all the events related here are truthful, because in our country violence has taken on a very big role with an average homicide rate of twelve deaths per day.

Sincerely, the Calderón Valladares Family

[*Signature*]	[*Signature*]
Victor Calderón Valladares	Diana Carolina
I.D. # 03418066-2	I.D. # 03617378-4

Translator's Note: A poorly written letter with insufficient punctuation. It was difficult to tell who did what to whom.

Rosetta Stone Translations, Tucson
Tel 520 575 9200 • rosettrans@aol.com • www.rosettrans.com

1

Abril 20, 2018

El salvador, San Salvador.

A quien interese.

Por medio de la presente carta nosotros la familia Calderón Valladares damos fé de los episodios traumáticos que tuvimos que enfrentar con la desaparición y asesinato de nuestras hermanas Karen y Leslie Valladares y siendo testigo de las amenazas que recibió mi hermano Wuiliam Calderón y su familia queremos expresar nuestro temor ya que ellos no pueden regresar a nuestro país porque pueden ser asesinados por los grupos terroristas que se escudan bajo nombres de pandillas que son individuos sin escrúpulos ni valores le acosaban a él y su familia por el hecho de trabajar en una dependencia del gobierno, le mantenían amenazado y bajo un constante soborno monetario, fuimos testigos del acto de violencia en contra de él su familia, en el que por auxiliar a su hija de un individuo que la detuvo y la toco a lo que ella llorando expresó los abusos que él cometió, su padre al tratar de ayudarla fue interceptado por otros tres sujetos que le esperaban escondidos en la oscuridad obstaculizando así su camino hacia su hija que gritaba por ayuda. Los sujetos lo tiraron al suelo pateandolo lo inmovilizaron y uno de ellos el cual portaba un arma de fuego lo toco con ella en la frente acusándolo de dar información a unos i9 investigadores que habían ingresado a su zona de residencia y capturado miembros pertenecientes a su institución, le amenazaron de muerte diciéndole que él y su familia iban a morir en sus manos por órdenes de sus superiores y que si él ponía una denuncia no serviría de nada puesto que ellos tienen infiltrados en la policía, fueron hechos muy traumantes para la familia Calderón, por eso expresamos nuestro temor y damos nuestra palabra de que todos los actos narrados en este medio son verídicos ya que en nuestro país la violencia ha tomado un papel muy grande teniendo una tasa promedio de doce muertes diarias.

Atentamente la familia Calderón Valladares.

Victor Calderón
Valladares
Dui # 03418066-2.

Diana Carolina

Dui # 03617378-

4

ROSETTA STONE *ASSOCIATES IN TRANSLATION*
7375 N. Calle sin Celo, Tucson, AZ 85718 • (520) 575-9200 • rosettrans@aol.com • www.rosettrans.com
• ATA-Certified •

Certification

AT THE REQUEST OF THE INTERESTED PARTY, I hereby certify that I have translated the following document:

Statement dated April 20, 2018 by Calderón Valladares family

from the Spanish into the English language on this 3rd day of July 2019, and that the information contained in the translated document is a true, complete and correct reflection of the original text, to the best of my ability as a Professional Translator.

ROSETTA STONE ASSOCIATES IN TRANSLATION

Carola P. Myers

CAROLA P. MYERS
Member, A.C.I.A. - ATA-Accredited

EXHIBIT '15':
Autopsy Documents of Lesia Liliana Quijada Valladares

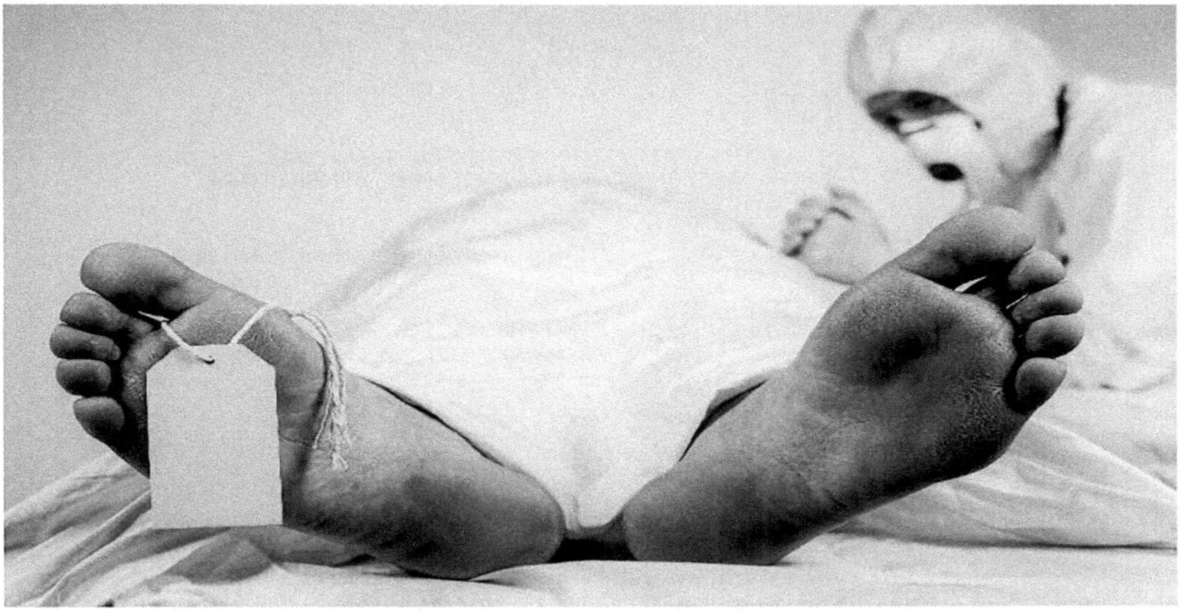

Translation from Spanish
3 July 2019

OFFICE OF THE ATTORNEY GENERAL OF THE REPUBLIC
SPECIAL INVESTIGATING UNIT FOR OFFENSES OF ORGANIZED CRIME

San Salvador, April 20, 2012

OFFICIAL LETTER No. 1596 URGENT.
Investigative Reference No. 202-CO-2011

Director
Institute of Forensic Medicine
Dr. Roberto Masferrer
Santa Tecla Region

I respectfully request that you order the appropriate personnel to **PROCEED TO IDENTIFY** the UNIDENTIFIED body of the victim on whom an ANTROPOLOGICAL STUDY was performed under the **Reference No. 19-2012-ST** for **CADAVER "A"** found on **03/15/2012** on an **UNNUMBERED LOT in COLONIA GRANADOS, CANTON ENTRE RIOS, MUNICIPALITY OF COLON, PROVINCE OF LA LIBERTAD**, as per the **Report of Biological Investigation of Criminology Number 159-12**, conducted by the Forensic Genetics Laboratory of the Institute of Forensic Medicine "Dr. Roberto Masferrer."

Thus, in view of the results of the comparative ADN test performed by the Genetics Lab of this Institution, where samples taken from Mrs. PAULA GILMA VALLADARES (the presumed mother) were compared with samples taken from the aforementioned body, as a result of which it was concluded that the PROBABILITY OF MATERNITY IS 99.9999%, which agrees with HUMMEL's verbal pronouncements that the MATERNITY is PRACTICALLY PROVEN WITH POSITIVE IDENTIFICATION, I request that you formally proceed to identify said body as **LESLIA LILIANA QUIJADA VALLADARES, born in Santa Tecla, La Libertad Province, on December 11, 1996, daughter of José Margarito Quijada and Paula Gilma Valladares**; and upon conclusion of this procedure, that you **release the aforesaid body to FRANCISCA ADRIANA VALLADARES, holder of I.D. card No. 01689739-2. The DNA analysis is enclosed.**

This is brought to your attention for all pertinent legal effects.

ATTORNEY GENERAL OFFICE OF THE REPUBLIC
SPECIAL INVESTIGATIVE UNIT
ORGANIZED CRIME OFFENSES
EL SALVADOR

GOD UNION LIBERTY

[Signature]
EUGENIA MARIA CASTRO MAYORGA
Prosecutor, Special Investigating Unit for Offenses of Organized Crime

Rosetta Stone Translations, Tucson
Tel 520 575 9200 • rosettrans@aol.com • www.rosettrans.com

FISCALIA GENERAL DE LA REPUBLICA
UNIDAD FISCAL ESPECIALIZADA DELITOS CONTRA CRIMEN ORGANIZADO

San Salvador, 20 de Abril de 2012.-

OFICIO No. 1596
Referencia Fiscal No. 202-CO-2011.-

URGENTE.-

Señor Director
Instituto de Medicina Legal
Dr. Roberto Masferrer.
Regional Santa Tecla.-

Atentamente, solicito que ordene a quien corresponda se **PROCEDA A IDENTIFICAR** el cuerpo SIN IDENTIDAD de la víctima cuyo ESTUDIO ANTROPOLOGICO fue realizado con la referencia Número **19-2012-ST**, que corresponde al **CADAVER "A"** que fue encontrado el día **15/03/2012** en **LOTE SIN NUMERO DE LA COLONIA GRANADOS, CANTON ENTRE RIOS, MUNICIPIO DE COLON, DEPARTAMENTO DE LA LIBERTAD**, según **informe de Investigación Biológica de Criminalística Número 159-12**, efectuado por el Laboratorio de Genética Forense del Instituto de Medicina Legal "Dr. Roberto Masferrer".

Por lo que visto el resultado de la prueba comparativa de A.D.N. practicada por el Laboratorio de Genética de ese Instituto, en donde se analizaron las muestras tomadas a la señora PAULA GILMA VALLADARES (supuesta madre), con las muestras tomadas del cadáver antes mencionado, producto del cual se ha concluido que la PROBABILIDAD DE MATERNIDAD ES DE L 99.9999%, que corresponden según los predicados verbales de HUMMEL A MATERNIDAD PRACTICAMENTE PROBADA CON IDENTIFICACION POSITIVA, solicito proceda formalmente a la identificación de dicho cadáver como **LESLIA LILIANA QUIJADA VALLADARES**, originaria de **Santa Tecla, Departamento de La Libertad**, en donde naciera el día **11 de diciembre de 1996**, hija de **Jose Margarito Quijada y de Paula Gilma Valladares**; y concluido el procedimiento anterior, se **entregue dicho cadáver a FRANCISCA ADRIANA VALLADARES**, titular del **DUI No. 01689739-2. Anexo análisis de ADN.**

Lo que hago de su conocimiento para los efectos legales pertinentes.

DIOS UNION LIBERTAD

FISCALIA GENERAL DE LA REPUBLICA · UNIDAD FISCAL ESPECIALIZADA DELITOS DE CRIMEN ORGANIZADO · EL SALVADOR

EUGENIA MARIA CASTRO MAYORGA
Fiscal Unidad Especializada contra El Crimen Organizado

ROSETTA STONE *ASSOCIATES IN TRANSLATION*
7375 N. Calle sin Celo, Tucson, AZ 85718 • (520) 575-9200 • rosettrans@aol.com • www.rosettrans.com
• ATA-Certified •

Certification

AT THE REQUEST OF THE INTERESTED PARTY, I hereby certify that I have translated the following document:

Letter requesting autopsy of Leslia Liliana Quijada Valladares

from the Spanish into the English language on this 3rd day of July 2019, and that the information contained in the translated document is a true, complete and correct reflection of the original text, to the best of my ability as a Professional Translator.

ROSETTA STONE ASSOCIATES IN TRANSLATION

Carola P. Myers

CAROLA P. MYERS
Member, A.C.I.A. - ATA-Accredited

Translation from Spanish
3 July 2019

INSTITUTE OF FORENSIC MEDICINE
"DR. ROBERTO MASFERRER"

NOTICE

[The Institute] CERTIFIES that in Colón, La Libertad,
on March fifteen, two thousand and twelve
at eleven hours and forty-five minutes, we identified the
body of Luslia Liliana Quijada Valladares
Address: Col. Granados, Canton of Entre Rios, Colón, La Libertad,

who according to the determination of the Medical Examiner assigned to the Institute of Forensic Medicine "Dr. Roberto Masferrer", died from:
Craniofacial injuries from bladed weapon
Was autopsy performed? YES or NO. The body is being released to
Francisca Adriana Valladares
I.D. # 01689739-2
This notice is being issued for burial purposes at:
Santa Tecla, at 13 hours and
-- minutes on this 20th day of
April, nineteen hundred and twelve.

Signed [Signature]
Dr. Oscar Armando Quijano Aguilar
Medical Examiner
Medical Supervisory Board # 4061

INSTITUTE OF FORENSIC MEDICINE DR. ROBERTO MASFERRER
CENTRAL REGION
Santa Tecla, El Salvador, C.A.

Rosetta Stone Translations, Tucson
Tel 520 575 9200 • rosettrans@aol.com • www.rosettrans.com

A

INSTITUTO DE MEDICINA LEGAL
"DR. ROBERTO MASFERRER"

ESQUELA

HACE CONSTAR: Que en Colon, L.L.

a las Once horas y cuarenta y cinco minutos, del dia quince

de marzo del año dos mil doce se ha reconocido el

cadáver de: Luslia Liliana Quijada Valladares.

Dirección: Col. Granados, ctón. Entierro, Colon, L.L

Quien según dictamen Médico Forense, adscrito al Instituto de Medicina Legal "Dr. Roberto Masferrer", falleció a consecuencia de: Traumas cranea faciales con arma blanca

Se practica autopsia SÍ o NO. El cadáver se entrega a: Francisco Adriana Valladares.

DUI # 01689739-2

Y para los efectos de inhumación se extiende la presente en: Santa Tecla, a las 13 horas y — minutos del día 20 de Abril del año dos mil doce.

F. Quijano

Dr. Oscar Armando Quijano Aguilar
Médico Forense
J.V.P.M. 4061

INSTITUTO DE MEDICINA LEGAL DR. ROBERTO MASFERRER

ROSETTA STONE *ASSOCIATES IN TRANSLATION*
7375 N. Calle sin Celo, Tucson, AZ 85718 • (520) 575-9200 • rosettrans@aol.com • www.rosettrans.com
• ATA-Certified •

Certification

AT THE REQUEST OF THE INTERESTED PARTY, I hereby certify that I have translated the following document:

Autopsy notice related to Luslía Liliana Quijada Valladares

from the Spanish into the English language on this 3rd day of July 2019, and that the information contained in the translated document is a true, complete and correct reflection of the original text, to the best of my ability as a Professional Translator.

ROSETTA STONE ASSOCIATES IN TRANSLATION

Carola P. Myers
CAROLA P. MYERS
Member, A.C.I.A. - ATA-Accredited

EXHIBIT '16':
Autopsy Documents of Karen Alejandra Valladares Zaldana

Translation from Spanish
3 July 2019

REPUBLIC OF EL SALVADOR IN CENTRAL AMERICA

OFFICE OF THE ATTORNEY GENERAL OF THE REPUBLIC
SPECIAL INVESTIGATING UNIT FOR OFFENSES OF ORGANIZED CRIME

San Salvador, April 20, 2012

<u>OFFICIAL LETTER No. 1597</u> <u>URGENT.</u>
Investigative Reference No. 202-CO-2011

Director
Institute of Forensic Medicine
Dr. Roberto Masferrer
Santa Tecla Region

I respectfully request that you order the appropriate personnel to **PROCEED TO IDENTIFY** the UNIDENTIFIED body of the victim on whom an ANTROPOLOGICAL STUDY was performed under the **Reference No. <u>20-2012-ST</u>** for **CADAVER "B"** found on **03/15/2012** on an **UNNUMBERED LOT** in **COLONIA GRANADOS, CANTON ENTRE RIOS, MUNICIPALITY OF COLON, PROVINCE OF LA LIBERTAD**, as per the **Report of Biological Investigation of Criminology Number 160-12**, conducted by the Forensic Genetics Laboratory of the Institute of Forensic Medicine "Dr. Roberto Masferrer."

Thus, in view of the results of the comparative ADN test performed by the Genetics Lab of this Institution, where samples taken from Mrs. PAULA GILMA VALLADARES (the presumed mother) were compared with samples taken from the aforementioned body, as a result of which it was concluded that the PROBABILITY OF MATERNITY IS 99.9999%, which agrees with HUMMEL's verbal pronouncements that the MATERNITY is PRACTICALLY PROVEN WITH POSITIVE IDENTIFICATION, I request that you formally proceed to identify said body as **KAREN ALEJANDRA VALLADARES ZALDAÑA, born in Santa Tecla, La Libertad Province, on May 17, 1993, daughter of Paula Gilma Valladares**; and upon conclusion of this procedure, that you **release the aforesaid body to FRANCISCA ADRIANA VALLADARES, holder of I.D. card No. 01689739-2. The DNA analysis is enclosed**.

This is brought to your attention for all pertinent legal effects.

ATTORNEY GENERAL OFFICE OF THE REPUBLIC
SPECIAL INVESTIGATIVE UNIT
ORGANIZED CRIME OFFENSES
EL SALVADOR, C.A.

GOD UNION LIBERTY

[Signature]
EUGENIA MARIA CASTRO MAYORGA
Prosecutor, Special Investigating Unit

Rosetta Stone Translations, Tucson
Tel 520 575 9200 • rosettrans@aol.com • www.rosettrans.com

FISCALIA GENERAL DE LA REPUBLICA
UNIDAD FISCAL ESPECIALIZADA DELITOS CONTRA CRIMEN ORGANIZADO

San Salvador, 20 de Abril de 2012.-

<u>OFICIO No. 1597</u>
Referencia Fiscal No. 202-CO-2011.-

URGENTE.-

Señor Director
Instituto de Medicina Legal
Dr. Roberto Masferrer,
Regional Santa Tecla.-

Atentamente, solicito que ordene a quien corresponda se **PROCEDA A IDENTIFICAR** el cuerpo SIN IDENTIDAD de la víctima cuyo ESTUDIO ANTROPOLOGICO fue realizado con la **referencia Número <u>20-2012-ST</u>**, que corresponde al **CADAVER "B"** que fue encontrado el día **15/03/2012 en LOTE SIN NUMERO DE LA COLONIA GRANADOS, CANTON ENTRE RIOS, MUNICIPIO DE COLON, DEPARTAMENTO DE LA LIBERTAD**, según **Informe de Investigación Biológica de Criminalística Número 160-12**, efectuado por el Laboratorio de Genética Forense del Instituto de Medicina Legal "Dr. Roberto Masferrer".

Por lo que visto el resultado de la prueba comparativa de A.D.N. practicada por el Laboratorio de Genética de ese Instituto, en donde se analizaron las muestras tomadas a la señora PAULA GILMA VALLADARES (supuesta madre), con las muestras tomadas del cadáver antes mencionado, producto del cual se ha concluido que la PROBABILIDAD DE MATERNIDAD ES DE L 99.9999%, que corresponden según los predicados verbales de HUMMEL A MATERNIDAD PRACTICAMENTE PROBADA CON IDENTIFICACION POSITIVA, solicito proceda formalmente a la Identificación de dicho cadáver como **KAREN ALEJANDRA VALLADARES ZALDAÑA**, **originaria de Santa Tecla, Departamento de La Libertad, en donde naciera el día 17 de mayo de 1993, hija de Paula Gilma Valladares;** y concluido el procedimiento anterior, **se entregue dicho cadáver a FRANCISCA ADRIANA VALLADARES, titular del DUI No. 01689739-2. Anexo análisis de ADN.**

Lo que hago de su conocimiento para los efectos legales pertinentes.

DIOS UNION LIBERTAD

FISCALIA GENERAL DE LA REPUBLICA · EL SALVADOR, C.A. · UNIDAD FISCAL ESPECIALIZADA DELITOS DE CRIMEN ORGANIZADO

EUGENIA MARIA CASTRO MAYORGA
Unidad Especializada contra El Crimen Organizado

ROSETTA STONE *ASSOCIATES IN TRANSLATION*

7375 N. Calle sin Celo, Tucson, AZ 85718 • (520) 575-9200 • rosettrans@aol.com • www.rosettrans.com
• ATA-Certified •

Certification

AT THE REQUEST OF THE INTERESTED PARTY, I hereby certify that I have translated the following document:

Letter requesting autopsy of Karen Alejandra Valladares Zaldaña

from the Spanish into the English language on this 3rd day of July 2019, and that the information contained in the translated document is a true, complete and correct reflection of the original text, to the best of my ability as a Professional Translator.

ROSETTA STONE ASSOCIATES IN TRANSLATION

Carola P. Myers

CAROLA P. MYERS
Member, A.C.I.A. - ATA-Accredited

Translation from Spanish
3 July 2019

INSTITUTE OF FORENSIC MEDICINE
"DR. ROBERTO MASFERRER"

NOTICE

[The Institute] CERTIFIES that in *Colón, La Libertad,*
on *March fifteen,* two thousand and *twelve*
at *twelve* hours and *..* minutes, we identified the
body of *Karen Alejandra Valladares Zaldoña*
Address: *Col. Granados, Canton of Entre Rios, Colón, La Libertad,*

who according to the determination of the Medical Examiner assigned to the Institute of Forensic Medicine "Dr. Roberto Masferrer", died from:
Craniofacial and cervical injuries from bladed weapon
Was autopsy performed? YES or NO. The body is being released to
Francisca Adriana Valladares
I.D. # 01689739-2
This notice is being issued for burial purposes at:
Santa Tecla, at *13* hours and
10 minutes on this *20th* day of
April, nineteen hundred and *twelve.*

Signed [*Signature*]
Dr. Oscar Armando Quijano Aguilar
Medical Examiner
Medical Supervisory Board # 4061

INSTITUTE OF FORENSIC MEDICINE DR. ROBERTO MASFERRER
CENTRAL REGION
Santa Tecla
El Salvador, C.A.

Rosetta Stone Translations, Tucson
Tel 520 575 9200 • rosettrans@aol.com • www.rosettrans.com

"B"

INSTITUTO DE MEDICINA LEGAL
"DR. ROBERTO MASFERRER"

ESQUELA

HACE CONSTAR: Que en Colon, L. L.
a las doce horas y — minutos, del día quince
de Marzo del año dos mil doce se ha reconocido el
cadáver de: Karen Alejandra Valladares Zaldaña
Dirección: Col. Granados, Cton. Entierros, Colon, L.L.

Quien según dictamen Médico Forense, adscrito al Instituto de Medicina Legal "Dr. Roberto Masferrer", falleció a consecuencia de:
Trauma craneofacial y cervical con arma blanca

Se practica autopsia SÍ o NO. El cadáver se entrega a:
Francisca Adriana Valladares
DUI # 01689739-2

Y para los efectos de inhumación se extiende la presente en: Santa Tecla, a las 13 horas y 10 minutos del día 20 de Abril del año dos mil doce.

F.
Dr. Oscar Armando Quijano Aguilar
Médico Forense
J.V.P.M. 4061

ROSETTA STONE *ASSOCIATES IN TRANSLATION*
7375 N. Calle sin Celo, Tucson, AZ 85718 • (520) 575-9200 • rosettrans@aol.com • www.rosettrans.com
• ATA-Certified •

Certification

AT THE REQUEST OF THE INTERESTED PARTY, I hereby certify that I have translated the following document:

Autopsy notice related to Karen Alejandra Valladares Zaldaña

from the Spanish into the English language on this 3rd day of July 2019, and that the information contained in the translated document is a true, complete and correct reflection of the original text, to the best of my ability as a Professional Translator.

ROSETTA STONE ASSOCIATES IN TRANSLATION

Carola P. Myers

CAROLA P. MYERS
Member, A.C.I.A. - ATA-Accredited

EXHIBIT '17':
Just Bones: Remains of Teen Victims Found in Clandestine Cemetery in La Libertad – El Salvador.com

Translation from Spanish
3 July 2019

JUST BONES

Remains of teen victims found in clandestine cemetery in La Libertad.

TODAY'S TOPIC

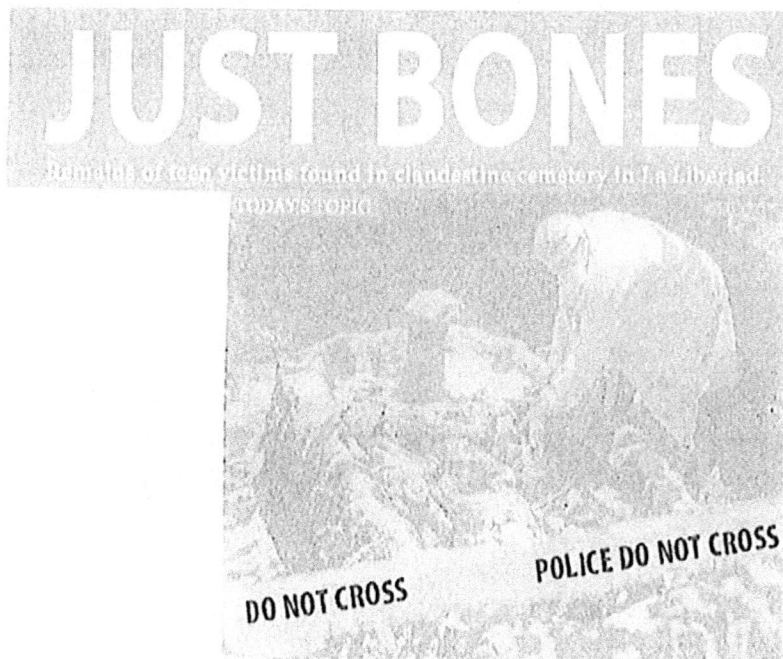

Two Sisters Found Buried in Secret Grave

• The victims disappeared in September 2011. They were students, age 14 and 18 years. • Eight members of the same family are also believed buried in this area.

Lilibeth Sánchez
Diana Escalante

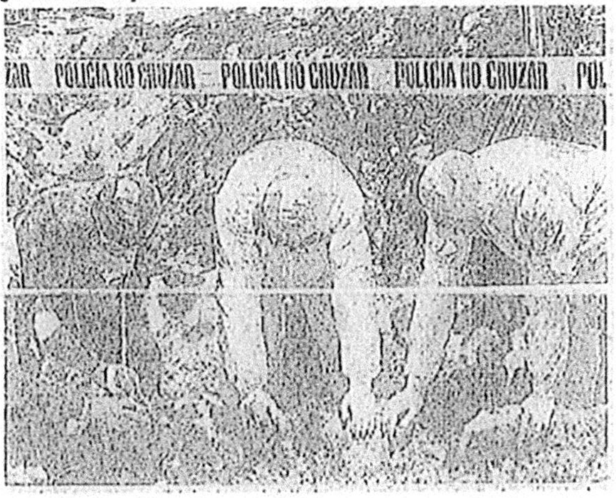

Criminalogist Israel Ticas and three investigators work to excavate the bodies of the sisters in the canton of Cinco Cedros, in Colón, La Libertad.

The mummified bodies of two sisters, age 14 and 18, missing since last September, were found yesterday in a clandestine cemetery in Colón, La Libertad.

Family members of the teens arrived in the borough of Granados in the canton of Cinco Cedros on hearing that the investigator Israel Ticas was excavating a grave in the area.

After the bodies were exhumed, the teens' family members were able to identify them based on their clothing, shoes and other accessories they had been wearing on the day the girls went missing.

However, sources from the Public Prosecutor's Office indicated they would ask the Institute of Forensic Medicine to conduct a DNA exam to confirm that these were really the missing sisters.

The victims were identified as Leslie Liliana, a seventh-grader at a local school, and Karen Alejandra, who was taking long-distance courses toward a bachelor's degree at a Santa Tecla school.

According to Ticas, the teens were killed with a pick because their faces were destroyed. He added that one of them also had been sexually assaulted by her killers.

The sisters were buried in the same area where in December, under the same circumstances,
Florencio Martinez

Gitón and Romeo Fermán were found, a driver and a fare collector on a Route 168 microbus, making trips between Santa Tecla and Quezaltepeque.

On December 9, the men made their customary roundtrip in the bus when a group of gang members stopped them, and together with the soldier Elder Valenzuela Bautista, a passenger on the bus, kidnapped and then killed them.

A Missing Family

The investigator from the Public Prosecutor's Office, Israel Ticas, confirmed yesterday that they would keep digging at the site over the next few days because they suspect that more bodies would be found there.

According to this specialist, among the victims who may be buried in the area —

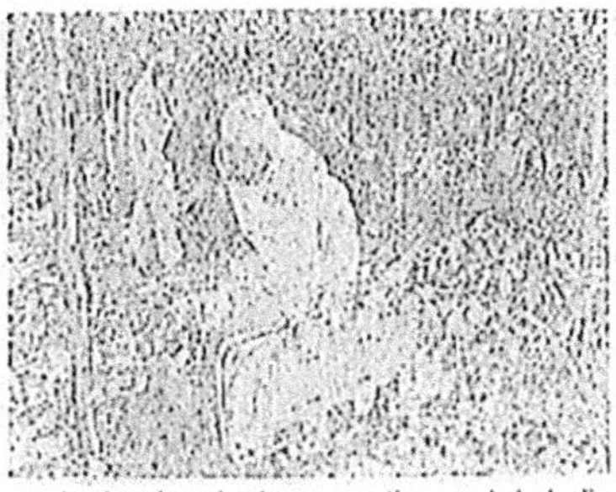

At the site where the sisters were discovered, the bodies of two Route 168 employees had been found in December.

where there is a strong presence of the Mara Salvatrucha — are eight members of the same family who last year disappeared in the Cinco Cedros canton from one day to the next.

The missing family, according to the information provided by the Authorities, consisted of four adults and four children (grandparents, parents, and children).

The investigator added that there are strong suspicions that the killers buried these eight individuals at the site in the same grave

Yesterday, Police were alerted by a phone call that some half-buried bones had been found in the Llano Verde borough in Ilopango. By closing time for this story, the Authorities have not provided any additional information on the case.

SOLO OSAMENTA

Hallan restos de jóvenes en cementerio clandestino en La Libertad.

DEPORTES!

¡Y OTRA BAILADA!

TEMA DEL DÍA

30 // NACIONAL

www.elsalvador.com • Viernes, 16 de m

Hallan sepultadas a dos hermanas en fosa clandestina

Las víctimas desaparecieron en septiembre de 2011. Eran estudiantes y tenían 14 y 18 años

Se presume que ocho miembros de una misma familia también están enterrados en la zona

Lilibeth Sánchez
Diana Escalante

Los cadáveres de dos hermanas de 14 y 18 años, quienes estaban desaparecidas desde septiembre pasado, fueron hallados ayer momificados en un cementerio clandestino de Colón, en La Libertad.

Parientes de las jóvenes llegaron hasta la colonia ...

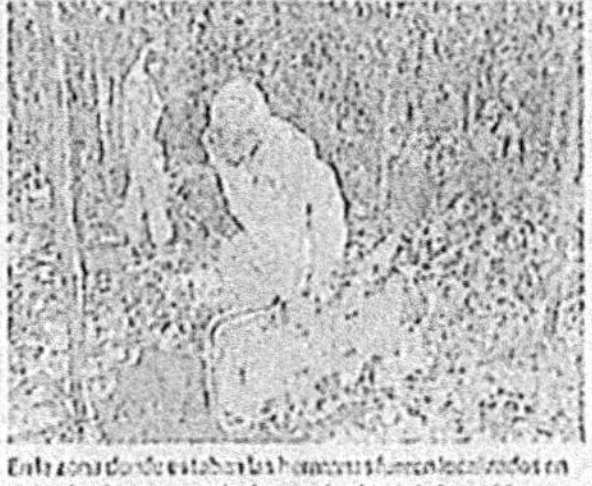

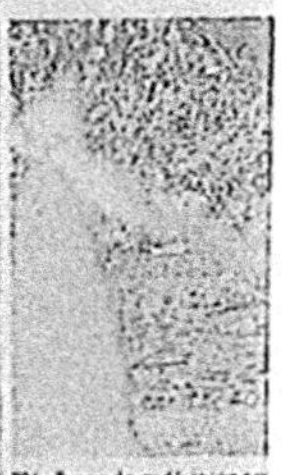

El hallazgo de cadáveres en ... hecho frecuente en el puent...

Hombre ... a su ex... luego s...

El crimen pasional ocurr... en Chalatenango. Un hombre también fue asesinado frente a la alcaldía de San Salvador

Diana Escalante
Lissette Abrego

ROSETTA STONE *ASSOCIATES IN TRANSLATION*

7375 N. Calle sin Celo, Tucson, AZ 85718 • (520) 575-9200 • rosettrans@aol.com • www.rosettrans.com
• ATA-Certified •

Certification

AT THE REQUEST OF THE INTERESTED PARTY, I hereby certify that I have translated the following document:

Newspaper report: Two Sisters Found Buried in Secret Grave

from the Spanish into the English language on this 3rd day of July 2019, and that the information contained in the translated document is a true, complete and correct reflection of the original text, to the best of my ability as a Professional Translator.

ROSETTA STONE ASSOCIATES IN TRANSLATION

Carola P. Myers

CAROLA P. MYERS
Member, A.C.I.A. - ATA-Accredited

Your Dependable Source of Foreign Language Translation and Interpretation

EXHIBIT '18':

Anda Employee Killed in Morazan – Diario 1.com

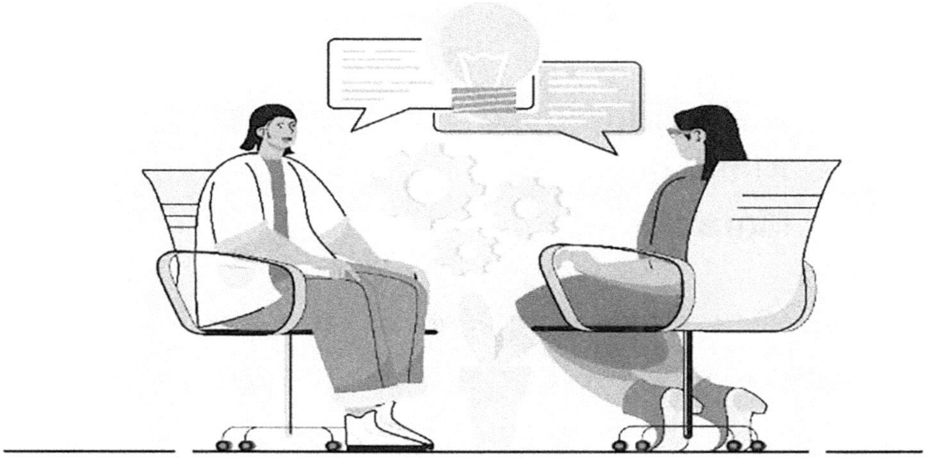

Image

ANDA Employee Killed in Morazán

According to Police, the man had previously been threatened by gang members; however, he had not reported it, so Police is not ruling out that the motive for the crime is related to this.

Reference image: D1

Juan Clímaco Anaya Nolasco, 40, a plumber and mechanic in charge of a tank pump and distribution wells for the National Administration of Aqueducts and Sewer Systems (ANDA), was killed this Thursday on the main street of the township of Sensembra, Province of Morazán, said the National Civil Police (PNC).

Reference image: D1

Juan Climaco Anaya Nolasco, 40, a plumber and mechanic in charge of a tank pump and distribution wells for the National Administration of Aqueducts and Sewer Systems (ANDA), was killed this Thursday on the main street of the township of Sensembra, Province of Morazán, said the National Civil Police (PNC).

Anaya Nolasco was as always headed to his place of work when he was intercepted by several gang members of the Seilor Locos Salvatruchos of the MS gang, said the Authorities.

The gang members surrounded the man and gave him a beating, and when he fell to the ground, already unconscious, they shot him several times until he was dead.

According to Police, the man had previously been threatened by gang members; however, he had not reported it, so Police is not ruling out that the motive behind the crime is related to this.

After the murder, the Authorities stated they would conduct the relevant investigations.

Image

Diario1.COM

Asesinan a empleado de ANDA en Morazán

La Policía señala que el hombre ya había sido amenazado por pandilleros; sin embargo, no puso la denuncia por lo que no descartan que el móvil del crimen esté relacionado.

Imagen de Referencia D1

Juan Clímaco Anaya Nolasco, de 40 años, quien era bombero y administrador de una bomba del tanque y de los pozos de distribución de la Administración Nacional de Acueductos y Alcantarillados (ANDA) [illegible]

Diario1.COM

Imagen de Referencia. D1

Juan Clímaco Anaya Nolasco, de 40 años, quien era fontanero y administrador de una bomba del tanque y de los pozos de distribución de la Administración Nacional de Acueductos y Alcantarillados (ANDA) fue asesinado este jueves en la calle principal del municipio de Sensembra, departamento de Morazán informó la Policía Nacional Civil (PNC).

Anaya Nolasco como era costumbre se dirigía hacia su lugar de trabajo cuando fue Interceptado por varios pandilleros de la clica Seilor Locos Salvatruchos de la MS, Indicaron las autoridades

Los pandilleros habrían rodeado al hombre y le propinaron una paliza, cuando cayó al suelo ya inconsciente, le dispararon varias veces hasta provocarle la muerte.

La Policía señala que Anaya Nolasco ya había sido amenazado por pandilleros; sin embargo, no puso la denuncia por lo que no descartan que el móvil del crimen esté relacionado.

Tras el asesinato las autoridades manifestaron que realizarán las investigaciones correspondientes.

ROSETTA STONE *ASSOCIATES IN TRANSLATION*
7375 N. Calle sin Celo, Tucson, AZ 85718 • (520) 575-9200 • rosettrans@aol.com • www.rosettrans.com
• ATA-Certified •

Certification

AT THE REQUEST OF THE INTERESTED PARTY, I hereby certify that I have translated the following document:

Newspaper report: ANDA Employee killed in Morazán

from the Spanish into the English language on this 3rd day of July 2019, and that the information contained in the translated document is a true, complete and correct reflection of the original text, to the best of my ability as a Professional Translator.

ROSETTA STONE ASSOCIATES IN TRANSLATION

Carola P. Myers

CAROLA P. MYERS
Member, A.C.I.A. - ATA-Accredited

Your Dependable Source of Foreign Language Translation and Interpretation

EXHIBIT '19':

Gang Members Kill Anda Employee – Elblog.com

Gang Members Kill Employ ..

ElBlog MENU

Gang Members Kill ANDA Employee

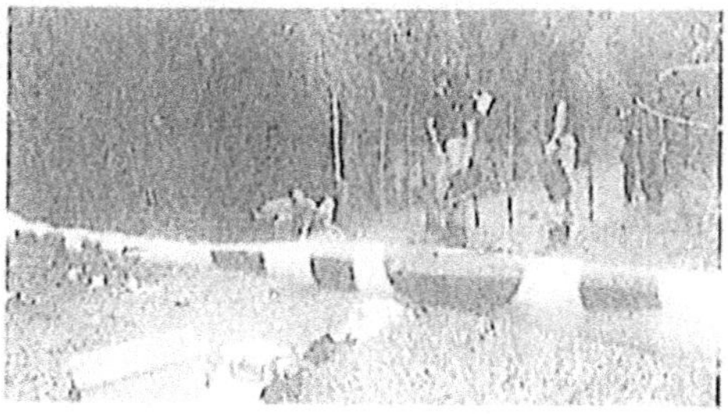

Editor's Blog
IN THE NEWS

The Authorities are investigating what brought about the attack on the public employee.

33% 10:28 p.m.

Gang Members Kill Employ ..

elblog.com

A man was killed early this Thursday by presumed gang members in the Miraflores borough of San Pedro Masahuat, La Paz.

According to the Authorities, the man worked for the National Administration of Aqueducts and Sewer Systems (ANDA), and was attacked as he was on his way to be seen at a local clinic.

At this time, the Authorities are investigating the motive for the killing. We have learned unofficially that one of his daughters was being harassed by gang members, and he was defending her, which could have provoked the attack.

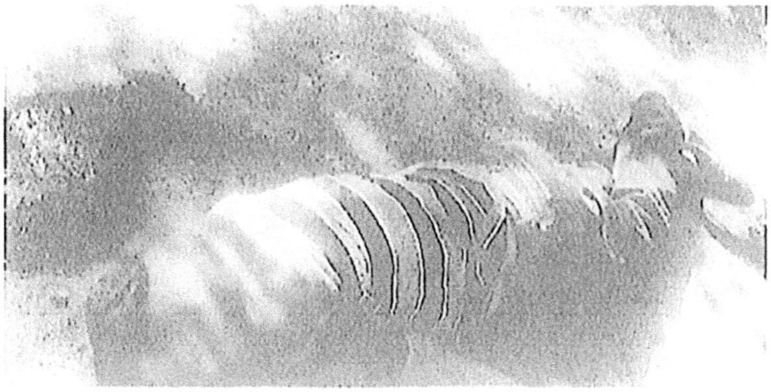

10:28 p. m.

Pandilleros asesinan a emplead...

elblog.com

El Blog

MENU

Pandilleros asesinan a empleado de ANDA

Redacción El Blog

EN NOTICIAS

Las autoridades investigan qué originó el ataque hacia el

33% 10:28 p. m.

Pandilleros asesinan a emplead...

elblog.com

Un hombre fue asesinado por presuntos pandilleros, la mañana de este jueves, en la colonia Miraflores de San Pedro Masahuat, La Paz.

De acuerdo con las autoridades, el hombre trabajaba para la Administración Nacional de Acueductos y Alcantarillados (ANDA) y fue atacado cuando se conducía a pasar consulta en una clínica del lugar.

Hasta el momento, las autoridades investigan el móvil del asesinato. Extraoficialmente se afirma, que una de sus hijas estaba siendo acosada por pandilleros y este la defendió, lo que puedo originar el ataque.

ROSETTA STONE ASSOCIATES IN TRANSLATION

7375 N. Calle sin Celo, Tucson, AZ 85718 • (520) 575-9200 • rosettrans@aol.com • www.rosettrans.com
• ATA-Certified •

Certification

AT THE REQUEST OF THE INTERESTED PARTY, I hereby certify that I have translated the following document:

Newspaper report: Gang Members Kill ANDA Employee

from the Spanish into the English language on this 3rd day of July 2019, and that the information contained in the translated document is a true, complete and correct reflection of the original text, to the best of my ability as a Professional Translator.

ROSETTA STONE ASSOCIATES IN TRANSLATION

Carola P. Myers

CAROLA P. MYERS
Member, A.C.I.A. - ATA-Accredited

Your Dependable Source of Foreign Language Translation and Interpretation

EXHIBIT '20':
MS-13 Threatens the Legitimacy of Salvadoran Government – The Heritage Foundation – 07/19/2018

COMMENTARY Global Politics

MS-13 Threatens the Legitimacy of Salvadoran Government

Jul 19th, 2018 3 min read

Commentary By

Ana Quintana

Senior Policy Analyst, Latin America and the Western Hemisphere

Macarena Martinez

Summer 2018 member of the Young Leaders Program at The Heritage Foundation

KEY TAKEAWAYS

In a recent poll, residents of El Salvador were asked, "Who runs your country?" Forty-two percent reported gangs, while only 12 percent said the government.

In recent years, MS-13 has launched minor programs to feed children and provide neighborhood security.

Failure to step up, create economic opportunities, and increase security efforts could collapse what remains of the Salvadoran government's authority.

In a recent poll, residents of El Salvador were asked, "Who runs your country?" Forty-two percent reported gangs, while only 12 percent said the government.

These results reveal a huge problem for El Salvador: The public's lack of trust in its government threatens to dismantle the country's democracy and stability.

MS-13 is a dominant force in Salvadoran affairs. Outside the U.S., MS-13's largest presence is in Central America, particularly in the northern triangle countries of El Salvador, Guatemala, and Honduras.

MS-13 has become a powerful force, capable of coercing weak Central American governments. For example, in 2012, the Salvadoran government was forced to sign a truce with MS-13 in an effort to reduce skyrocketing homicide rates. Although the truce did reduce homicides, the agreement was widely unpopular. Extortion and associated criminal activity continued at high rates with almost no resistance from the government.

When current President Salvador Sánchez Cerén reversed the 2012 truce and implemented a "mano dura," or iron-first policy, against MS-13 in 2014, the gang retaliated by dumping bodies on the streets. The homicide rate skyrocketed and in 2015, El Salvador had the highest homicide rate in the world.

MS-13 largely relies on extortion as its largest source of income, but has also been known to engage in drug and human trafficking, money laundering, kidnapping, and theft. MS-13's growing influence in El Salvador has led to changes in its behavior.

The country's weak state capacity and inability to deliver social services has paved the way for criminal organizations to step in and assume state functions.

In recent years, MS-13 has launched minor programs to feed children and provide neighborhood security. Bizarrely, the same group that terrorized Salvadorans is now providing much-needed social services.

This change in behavior has undermined the Salvadoran government's authority. Fragile States Index tracked the public's perception of the state's legitimacy. El Salvador saw its sharpest decline in 2015, and perceived authority has continued to plummet ever since.

In 2017, Transparency International's corruption perception score for El Salvador ticked downward 6 points from 2014, indicating an increased corruption perception. Furthermore, El Salvador scored a 33 out of 100 in the country's perceived level of public-sector corruption.

In The Heritage Foundation's Index of Economic Freedom, El Salvador's government integrity score plummeted from 39 percent in 2016 to 25.2 percent in 2018—a clear indication of a serious problem.

Improving the situation will require long-term efforts from the Salvadoran government. Much of the work will be up to the next administration that will take office in 2019. It will be left to vigorously combat the expansion of MS-13 and preserve the government's legitimacy.

Failure to step up, create economic opportunities, and increase security efforts could collapse what remains of the Salvadoran government's authority.

This piece originally appeared in The Daily Signal

EXHIBIT '21':

El Salvador's Politics of Perpetual Violence – Genocide Watch – 12/19/2017

GENOCIDEWATCH

Genocide Watch exists to predict, prevent, stop, and punish genocide and other forms of mass murder. Our purpose is to build an international movement to prevent and stop genocide.

Search Site

TAKE ACTION

Home About Us The Call Ten Stages Alerts About Genocide Issues Alliance Get Involved

EL SALVADOR

EL SALVADOR'S POLITICS OF PERPETUAL VIOLENCE

Share

Tweet

December 19, 2017 | International Crisis Group

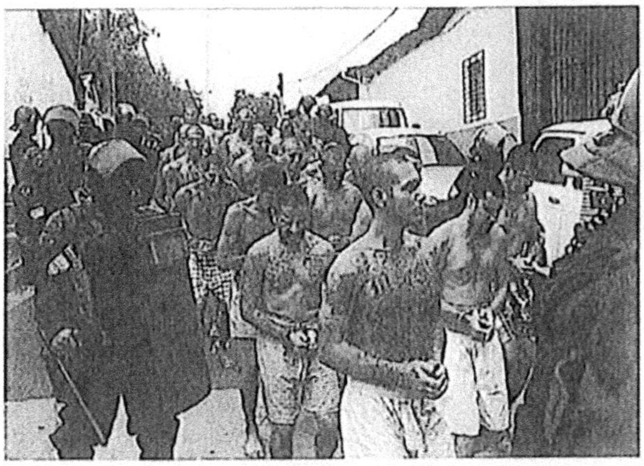

- What's the issue? After fifteen years of failed security policies, the government of El Salvador and criminal gangs are deadlocked in an open confrontation. Efforts aimed at tackling the deep-rooted social issues behind the gang phenomenon have not produced desired results due to a lack of political commitment and social divisions that gangs use to their advantage.

- Why does it matter? Born in the wake of U.S. deportation policies in the late 90s, gang violence in El Salvador has developed into a national security problem that accounts for the country's sky-high murder rate. The combination of mano dura (iron fist) policies and the U.S. administration's approach to migration could worsen El Salvador's already critical security situation.

- What should be done? All political actors should honour the government's holistic violence prevention strategies by fully implementing them and reframing anti-gang policies. Specific police and justice reforms, as well as a legal framework for rehabilitating former gang members, are crucial steps toward a future pacification process.

Executive Summary

El Salvador, a small country in the isthmus of Central America, is wracked by an implacable strain of gang warfare. Exceptionally intense and persistent violence pits rival street gangs against one another and in opposition to the police and state. Formerly hailed for its smooth transition to democracy and for turning the two foes of its 1980s civil war into political forces competing vigorously yet peaceably for power, El Salvador once again is famed for its bloodletting. Its recent murder rates rank among the highest in the world and its jails are among the most overcrowded. For the administration of U.S. President Donald Trump, its main gang, the Mara Salvatrucha (MS-13), personifies the menace of undocumented immigration. Although the Salvadoran state has developed a series of strategies for violence prevention, its mainly repressive efforts over the past fifteen years have checked the influence of these alternative approaches. It should now implement plans to prevent crime, rehabilitate gang members and spur development in marginalised communities. Most urgently, El Salvador will require protection from the turbulence that U.S. mass deportations could provoke.

The permanence of violence owes as much to the success as to the failings of the peace accords. The two former wartime foes have jostled for democratic supremacy, repeatedly using security policy for electoral purposes by seeking to satisfy public demand for mano dura (iron fist) against the gangs. Although government has changed hands, security methods have not altered: mass detentions and incarceration, as well as militarisation of policing, have become standard procedure whether under the rule of right-wing elites or former guerrillas. U.S. authorities have recently offered support to this approach, pledging to "dismantle" the MS-13.

In private, however, high-level officials from across the country's political divide lament the harmful effects of this crackdown on overstretched courts and front-line police. Blueprints geared to preventing the drift of young men from low-income neighbourhoods into gang life have been drafted; the government launched the most recent, the "Safe El Salvador" plan, as a holistic strategy to restore the state's territorial control. But as violence soared after 2014 following the disintegration of a truce with the gangs, extreme measures of jail confinement and police raids have once again become the government's predominant methods to choke the gangs. Allegations of police brutality and extrajudicial executions have multiplied.

Recent surveys suggest that veteran members of these gangs wish to cease the violence. However, the economic dividend of El Salvador's urban outskirts – the country's recent GDP growth rate of 1.9 per cent is among the lowest in Central America – continues to drive a supply of willing young recruits, and consolidate a vanguard of sympathisers dependent on income from the gangs' extortion schemes and other rackets. The reality and stigma of gang violence combine to block off alternative ways of life for those born into these communities, cutting years of schooling for young people in areas of high gang presence and alienating potential employers. Instead of succumbing to the state's offensive, gangs set up roadblocks in their neighbourhoods and impose their own law; their fight against security forces has claimed the lives of 45 police officers so far this year.

The deadlock between a tarnished set of sec[illegible]cies and a gang phenomenon that thrives on the ostracism and contemp[illegible]nstream Salvadoran society can only now be resolved by recasting the way the co[illegible]ts its security dilemmas. Judicial and security institutions require carefu[illegible] to ensure resources are distributed to areas with the highest concentrations of violen[illegible], and used to boost intelligence-led policing that targets gang members comm[illegible]g the most serious crimes. Jail based reinsertion schemes, and cooperation with diverse churches, NGOs and businesses that offer second chances to former gang members, must be strengthened to provide a legal framework for rehabilitation as well as material incentives for the gangs to eventually disband. Although the country's main political parties and most of the public oppose any hint of negotiation with gangs, the reality in many poor areas is of constant daily encounters with these groups. Tolerance for these grassroots efforts, despite the existing legal restrictions on any contact with gangs, is essential to build the confidence that will be required for dialogue in the future.

None of this will be easy, nor is it likely to be assisted by U.S. policy toward either gangs or Salvadoran immigrants. The potential cancellation of the rights to residency in the U.S. of 195,000 beneficiaries of the Temporary Protected Status (TPS) program threatens to overwhelm the Salvadoran state's capacity to accommodate returnees, not unlike the experience of the late 1990s when mass deportations of gang members from the U.S. to El Salvador exported the criminal capital that led to the lightning rise of the MS-13 and its main rival, the 18th Street gang. El Salvador is simply unprepared, economically and institutionally, to receive such an influx, or to handle their 192,700 U.S. children, many of them at the perfect age for recruitment or victimisation by gangs. At a time when levels of violence remain extraordinarily high, with exhaustion toward an unwinnable conflict voiced on both sides, the arrival of thousands of migrants back to their crime-affected homeland would impose huge strains. To escape its perpetual violence, El Salvador needs support, not the recurrence of past mistakes.

Recommendations

To improve El Salvador's public policies on security and prevent further regional spillover of gang violence and undocumented migration

To the government of El Salvador:

1. Fully implement the five axes of "Plan Safe El Salvador", and balance investment between law enforcement, institutional strengthening and violence prevention.

2. Approve a legal framework for rehabilitation, with special emphasis on the reinsertion of former gang members into society in coordination with local NGOs and the church.

3. Recognise the existence of forced displacement in El Salvador, adopt the Comprehensive Regional Framework for Protection and Solutions (MIRPS), and work in coordination with local NGOs to implement protection mechanisms for its victims.

4. Allow visits from humanitarian organisations to high security jails.

5. Institutionalise by executive order monthly meetings between the security cabinet and human rights groups to monitor alleged violations of human rights by security forces.

6. Create stronger coordination protocols between the National Civil Police and the prosecutor's office, and strengthen the former's internal control unit to ensure those suspected of abuse or corruption are held accountable.

To members of El Salvador's Legislative Assembly:

1. Promote multiparty efforts on security and support the government in the implementation of "Plan Safe El Salvador".

2. Revise the distribution of resources in the judiciary to ensure they are based on intensity of criminal activity rather than administrative criteria.

3. Stabilise funding to the prosecutor's office by giving it a fixed percentage of the annual state budget, and mandate the office with monitoring forced disappearances.

To the government of the U.S.:

1. Avoid massive deportations, and redesignate El Salvador for Temporary Protected Status (TPS).

2. Continue providing El Salvador with financial support to carry out violence-prevention initiatives, and place a greater emphasis on investigative policing and general skills training in the security forces.

To El Salvador donor countries and institutions:

1. Promote creation of an independent observatory to provide monthly information on crime victims, gang expansion and homicide figures.

2. Finance a plan in coordination with the private sector to offer incoming youth deportees job skills and employment opportunities.

Guatemala City/Brussels, 19 December 2017

I Introduction

In January 2017, El Salvador's celebrated the 25th anniversary of the end of its civil war (1980-1992), which killed 70,000 people and displaced over a million. Sealing the end of the conflict, the 1992 Chapultepec Peace Accords enabled the former guerrilla Farabundo Martí National Liberation Front(FMLN) to transform into a political party, and created a new civilian police force. Since then, El Salvador has remained among the most politically stable countries in Latin America, with two main parties that are heirs to the two sides of the internecine conflict – the left-wing FMLN and the conservative National Republican Alliance (ARENA) – peacefully alternating in power. However, the country's post-war political and security institutions have proved singularly unable to respond to an evolving and expanding criminal landscape. The country has suffered at least 93,000 murders since 1993, over half of which can be attributed to gangs. These groups now have around 60,000 active members and an estimated social support base of 500,000 – 8 per cent of El Salvador's 6.2 million population – making them the largest criminal organisations in Central America. Although gangs such as the Mara Salvatrucha (MS-13) and the two factions of 18th Street gang have a worldwide presence, their violent behaviour in El Salvador constitutes a national security crisis. Gangs control an undefined number of informal settlements and urban outskirts all over the country, and finance themselves mostly through small-scale extortion. Since 2003, both FMLN and ARENA governments have anchored their anti-criminal policies in restoring full state control over territory with high gang presence, mass incarceration and joint police and military operations. The current fight against crime, unveiled in early 2015 by President Sánchez Cerén of the ruling FMLN party, is the latest in a long line of law enforcement campaigns, although this initiative places more emphasis than predecessors on violence prevention in selected municipalities. Yet past and present anti-gang policies have achieved little in terms of stemming violent crime, and in some cases have even contributed to gang recruitment, financial prowess and firepower. Between 2013 and 2015 El Salvador experienced its steepest escalation in violence since 1994, with 11,934 homicides in 2015 and 2016 combined, a 53 per cent increase in comparison to the 2013-2014 period.

Far from abating, El Salvador's extreme insecurity could well intensify in 2018 as a number of threats loom over the country and the Central American region as a whole. These include the potentially devastating shock of new U.S. migration policies, economic and financial strains, and the possibly disruptive interference by gangs in forthcoming local elections.

This report, Crisis Group's first ever publication on El Salvador, assesses the origins of the country's violence, as well as the characteristics of and motives behind past and present security strategies. Combining original quantitative analysis based on official violence and migration statistics from El Salvador and the U.S., as well as extensive fieldwork across the country, the report identifies the principal causes behind security policy failures and highlights opportunities for a more comprehensive and sustainable approach to crime reduction. Crisis Group conducted over 70 interviews with top-level government officials, grassroots NGOs, academics, humanitarian workers, diplomats, security experts, and victims living in gang-controlled areas. All fieldwork was carried out in the country's most violent areas, such as the capital San Salvador and the smaller municipalities of San Miguel and Santa Ana.

II State and Crime in El Salvador

Two strong political parties with deep social roots, a judicial system marked by an unequal distribution of resources, and a police force increasingly backed by military clout stand out among the main features of El Salvador's public security institutions. The MS-13 gang and the two factions of the 18th Street gang are the largest criminal groups operating in the country; their ability to inflict high levels of violence and intimidation is directly related to an increase in the number of internally displaced persons (IDPs), refugees and asylum seekers in the region.

A Security Policies and El Salvador's Two party System

El Salvador has a robust two-party system dominated by the FMLN and ARENA. The country's fourteen departments and 262 municipalities depend largely on the central government – controlled by the FMLN since 2009 – for the design and implementation of security policies. Most security powers fall under the remit of the Ministry of Justice and Public Security, which runs the police and the prison system. The country's parliament, the Legislative Assembly – dominated since 2012 by ARENA – has 84 deputies from five parties, and a specific committee overseeing security matters. Local governments have gained a greater say in recent years over the implementation of violence prevention initiatives, but their main role continues to be that of sustaining the parties' social support base in a context of constant electoral campaigning.

The FMLN and ARENA both draw on strong public roots and feature hierarchical structures and leadership cohorts that have remained largely intact for the last 25 years. The

FMLN has around 30 000 rank-and-file milita[illegible]st of them from urban areas. ARENA has more active affiliates, 50,000, w[illegible]pport base primarily located in rural municipalities. The two parties represent op[illegible]ocial and ideological poles. Whereas the FMLN still deploys revolutionary [illegible] and aligns itself with other left-wing political movements in the hemisphere, ARENA was founded as an anti-communist party and is backed by the country's economic and business elites. In both parties, decision-making is concentrated in a select circle of high-level figures, most of whom have been in charge since 1992.

Despite stark ideological differences, the main parties' approaches to security are surprisingly similar. From 1999 to 2009, ARENA based its anti-criminal strategy on swift judicial processes, more arrests and mass incarceration. The FMLN continued this punitive approach – especially since its second mandate started in 2014 – with even harsher confinement conditions for jailed gang members and an enhanced role for the military in public security. Since losing executive power, ARENA has expressed only modest opposition to decisions taken by the Security Cabinet, the highest authority on these issues. Its most prominent members are the Vice President and presidential appointee for security Óscar Ortiz, the Minister of Justice and Public Security Mauricio Rodríguez Landaverde, and the Director of the Police Howard Cotto.

However, decision-making on security and other national priorities has been handicapped in recent years by a divided Assembly controlled by ARENA, which has forced the FMLN to compromise and seek support from smaller groups. New parties such as the right-wing Great Alliance for National Unity (GANA) have benefited from this parliamentary blockage, with its leader Guillermo Gallegos elected president of the Legislative Assembly in 2015. Only a handful of cross-party agreements have been reached, while more than 25 negotiation attempts in key policy areas have collapsed. The most recent was a six-month UN-backed mission launched in January 2017 to mark the 25th anniversary of the end of the war, which failed to establish common ground between the main parties. The chief of mission, Mexican diplomat Benito Andión, finished the mandate in July 2017 concluding that "conditions [for consensus] were not met" in the current political climate.

The arrival of young leaders on the national political scene, and a sharp drop in popular support for both the FMLN and ARENA, could be the harbinger of a shift away from traditional two-party rule. "Around 40 to 50 per cent of the Salvadoran population have not made up their minds as to which party to vote for", affirms a San Salvador-based political analyst. The most well-known representatives of this younger political generation are San Salvador Mayor Nayib Bukele – who was expelled from the FMLN in October 2017 after a series of internal party squabbles – and Johnny Wright Sol, an ARENA lawmaker who opted not to stand for re-election in 2018 due to disagreements with the party's leadership. Both have announced they will stand as independent candidates in the 2019 presidential elections, when the strength of the main parties will be tested.

B.The Judicial System, Security Forces and Jails

The institutions in charge of investigating and trying crimes in El Salvador are the prosecutor's office, the police and the judiciary. The prosecutor's office (in Spanish Fiscalía General de la República) is part of the larger public ministry, while the judiciary is headed by the Supreme Court and its different chambers. Both are independent public powers. In contrast, the National Civil Police is run by the executive branch's Ministry of Justice and Public Security.

Saturation of courts and a chronic paucity of forensic evidence are common challenges for most Latin American judicial institutions, but in El Salvador extreme criminal violence and new norms of legal prosecution based on mass detentions have gravely undermined the country's courts. Since the distribution of judicial personnel is purely based on the country's administrative divisions, magistrates working in more violent areas process up to ten times more cases than colleagues in quieter municipalities. "[Our work] looks like a maquila [a factory that assembles goods]", explained a judge from San Salvador. Poor relations with the police undermine the prosecutor's office, spurring Attorney General Douglas Meléndez to demand that he be given his own investigative force. "We work with borrowed hands and teeth", said Meléndez in a July 2017 conference.

Meanwhile, the Salvadoran police have come under increasing pressure as it seeks to deal with demands to combat violent crime and armed attacks from gangs. The National Civil Police has 28 000 officers, around 90 per cent of whom come from humble social backgrounds, and the average salary is $424 per month. This forces many to live in gang-controlled areas, usually neighbourhoods with lower rents, putting them and their families at risk. Officers in the field describe feeling alone and emotionally exhausted during but also after work. "After work, when we become normal citizens, I feel vulnerable … I just had a colleague killed this week during his time off", said one police officer on the El Salvador-Guatemala border. Criminal groups reportedly killed 45 officers from 1 January to 6 December 2017.

Originally designed in the peace accord to have a community-oriented role, the rising gang presence has increasingly pushed the police force toward methods based on armed raids in gang-affected communities as well as direct confrontation and firefights. These rose from 256 in 2014 to 676 in 2015, leaving 93 officers and 359 alleged criminals dead. Human rights groups argue this increase conceals a wave of extrajudicial killings, and presented this data to the Inter-American Court of Human Rights in September 2017. Government authorities acknowledged there may be some cases of excesses or misconduct but said they were "personal decisions [by officers], not a state policy". However, several media outlets have published in-depth investigations of alleged massacres of suspected gang members, sexual abuse of minors and extortion. Although the police monitors alleged abuses, and senior security authorities meet monthly with human rights representatives to discuss relevant cases, NGOs have denounced lack of accountability for officers suspected of abuse.

The burdens on the police have pushed the military towards deeper involvement in public security issues, converting its participation in anti-crime operations into a semi-permanent strategy. The Salvadoran army is the national institution with the highest public approval rating, and included around 24,800 active members in 2011. It understands its security role as a temporary measure limited to following police orders. However, senior officers consider military involvement to have become normal procedure given the transformation of the gang phenomenon: "we operate in a grey area … the criminal problem in this country has turned from a public security to a national security issue".

Corruption is prevalent in Salvadoran judicial and security institutions, though this is also common in many Latin American countries. A total of 31 per cent of Salvadorans report having paid a bribe to access basic public services over the past year according a 2017 Transparency International study, below other countries in the region such as Mexico (51) or Panama (36). The lack of effective internal control mechanisms harms these bodies' reputation. Accountability in most cases relies on the individual probity and political will of high-level officials, who themselves are chosen by a majority vote of the Legislative Assembly. The case of former Attorney General Luis Martínez, detained by his successor Douglas Meléndez, illustrates alleged abuses of state power. Martínez was incarcerated in August 2016 on charges of conspiracy, litigation fraud and withholding evidence during his mandate, although he denies the accusations and so far has not been convicted of any crime.

At the end of the country's penal process stands a prison system that is among the world's most overcrowded. Fourteen prisons house approximately 39 000 inmates, of whom 26 000 have been sentenced and 13 000 are remanded in custody. This includes prisoners in police detention stations, some of them converted into longer-term facilities due to lack of space. Roughly 800 officers and prison guards watch over the jail population, far below the ideal ratio of public officials to prisoners. Some jails have been placed under a state of emergency since early 2016, when the government imposed harsh new confinement conditions on gang members. El Salvador's Human Rights Prosecutor and several NGOs have denounced "systematic human rights violations" in jails under the new measures. One prison officer described the sixth sector of Zacatecoluca prison, where the national leaders of the largest gangs are held, as follows: "[from that place] you either leave dead or demented … It scared the hell out of me".

C.Gang Violence and Homicide Rates

Gang violence is a regional phenomenon rooted in the countries of Central America's Northern Triangle, but which now has international reach. The largest, most violent groups are the MS-13 and the two factions of 18th Street gang (in Spanish Barrio 18): 18-Sureños and 18-Revolucionarios. The origin of these groups, and the long history of rivalry among them, can be traced back to emigrant Central American communities in 1980s California. After mass deportations from the U.S. in the late 1990s, Salvadoran gangs adopted U.S. gang culture and identity, and pioneered the expansion of MS-13 and the 18th Street gang in the early 2000s. These gangs have a worldwide presence of around 140,000 members, of whom 40 000 live in the U.S. and 100 000 are based in El Salvador, Honduras, Guatemala, Mexico and Italy.

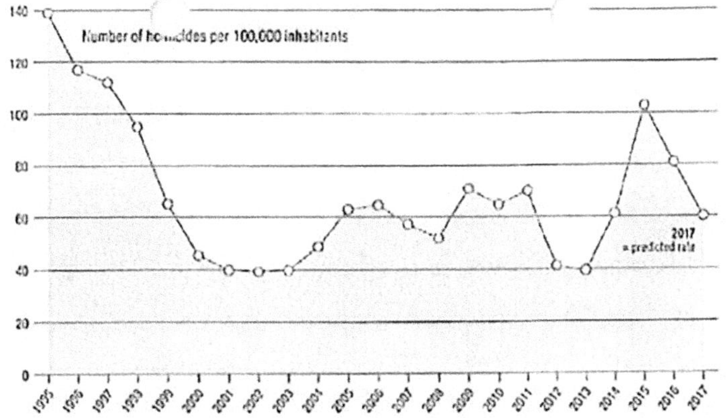

Figure 1. Homicide rates in municipalities with low and high gang presence and yearly criminal deportations from the U.S. National Civilian Police and U.S. Department of Homeland Security

1.The exceptional problem of gang violence in El Salvador

In light of El Salvador's size and population, the extent of gangs' territorial presence, as well as its armed power, has no equal anywhere in the world. The country has the largest number of active gang-members in the region, an estimated 60,000, which exceeds the approximately 52,000 Salvadoran police and military officers. The gang social support base rises to 500,000 people – almost 8 per cent of total population – including sympathisers and former members, or calmados (gang lexicon for those who have desisted from gang activities).

The typical profile of a gang member in El Salvador is a young male around 25 years old, born to a low-income, often broken family, who joined the gang at the age of fifteen. According to a March 2017 survey of over 1,000 jailed gang affiliates, most members came from marginalised neighbourhoods, and 70 per cent lived on less than $250 a month. The same study suggested that some 94 per cent do not have a secondary education, over 80 per cent have never held formal employment, and more than half come from families that had suffered a break-up.

The relationship between criminal activity and territorial presence is perhaps the most unique feature of the country's gang phenomenon. Gang revenues are drawn from extortion rackets and, to a lesser extent, drug-trafficking and sales. Gangs such the MS-13 gain up to $31.2 million per year from extorting 70 per cent of all the businesses in the territories where they are present, estimated at 247 out of the country's 262 municipalities. Most of their victims are small- and medium-sized business-owners, informal tradespeople and transport workers. Unlike their peers in Honduras, Salvadoran gangs do not have direct business control over parts of the drug trade, but have sub-contractual relationship with narco-traffickers, who employ them sporadically as muscle in some operations.

The response from the Salvadoran state to the gang threat has triggered major transformations inside these organisations. After 4,000 gang members were jailed between 2004 and 2008 – and segregated by rival groups to avoid violent clashes – gang leaders began to centralise operations and behave more like traditional criminal bosses. According to Jeannette Aguilar, a Salvadoran academic, "the rise of the jail population [after the first] anti-gang plans … enabled [these groups] to find in jails a suitable niche for their formalisation and institutionalisation, making jails their new spaces for territorial control". El Salvador's security policies in the 2000s, based on mass incarceration of suspected gang members, also helped gangs diversify their criminal activities – including extortion – by improving communication channels, and discouraging tattoos so as to avoid police identification.

A failed attempt at state-led indirect dialogue with gang leaders between 2012 and 2013 spurred the most recent transformation of Salvadoran gangs. The collapse of the truce led to "anarchy" inside gangs' neighbourhood cells, or clicas, as leaders were isolated in maximum security prisons after the implementation of "extraordinary measures" in mid-2016. According to various sources, gangs have intensified violence against public officials and expanded their presence into rural areas. Media investigations and testimony gathered by the prosecutor's office suggest that, in the run-up to the 2014 presidential elections, ARENA and FMLN party bosses allegedly paid gangs $350,000 in exchange for votes in territories under their control.

If true, the alleged deal – denied by both political parties – would point to gangs' extraordinary power to influence electoral processes and threaten candidates. Some local authorities fear ties between gangs and parties could also impinge on voting in upcoming polls. Many officials confirm in private that communication with gangs is inevitable. "Let's be honest, every single party in this country talks to gangs, how they would not, since they have to organise rallies in their territories?", said a veteran government official.

Although nowadays gangs appear more dangerous than ever, there are signs that a significant number of members would be willing to lay down arms. In January 2017, gangs released a joint communiqué a week before the 25th anniversary of the 1992 peace accords asking the government for a new dialogue process, and offering to disband. According to the previously mentioned survey, nearly 70 per cent of jailed gang members have intentions of leaving the group. The authors said respondents commonly gave personal reasons, such as becoming parents, surviving an attack or the effect of a friend's or relative's murder.

2.Beyond homicide rates

With a murder rate of 103 per 100,000 people, El Salvador became in 2015 the country with the highest murder rate in the world. This rise in homicides includes an increase in mass killings and femicides. According to a 2013 study by Fundaungo, a local think-tank, over half those killed between 2009 and 2012 were fifteen-34 years old, approximately 80 per cent of the victims were male, 70 per cent of the killings were carried out by firearms, and nearly 40 per cent took place in public spaces.
How many of these murders can be attributed to gang violence is in dispute. But by 2012, the predominant role of gang violence in the overall number of homicides has become much clearer. During the first months of negotiation with the gangs, killings fell by 40 per cent. This sudden drop suggested that by 2012 gang leaders had sufficient power over local branches to reduce killings sharply nationwide. Disappearances have also become a grave concern, even though no public institution in El Salvador systematically tracks these cases: between 2010 and 2016, the prosecutor's office received 23,000 reports of disappearances, and the police 11,252.
D.Criminal Violence and Migration

Central America is afflicted by a humanitarian crisis that has spread to the U.S. and Mexico. The number of refugees and asylum seekers from the three countries of the Northern Triangle of Central America (Guatemala, Honduras and El Salvador) has seen nearly a tenfold increase since 2011 according to the UN Refugee Agency (UNHCR). In 2016, UNHCR estimated that there were 164,000 refugees and asylum-seekers from Guatemala, Honduras and El Salvador combined, as well as 450,000 irregular crossings from these countries to Mexico. Since 2015, Mexico and Costa Rica have experienced a steep increase in asylum requests from Northern Triangle migrants. While migration in Central America has historically been tied to the search for economic opportunity, the recent spike in undocumented migration owes much to the flight from criminal violence. According to a May 2017 survey by Doctors Without Borders (MSF), nearly 40 per cent of asylum seekers from the Northern Triangle in Mexico mentioned direct attacks from criminal groups as a reason for fleeing.

The scope of the humanitarian emergency in El Salvador is hard to measure given the lack of official data on the number of internally displaced people (IDPs) – itself a reflection of the government's refusal to recognise this phenomenon even though the Supreme Court of Justice and the human rights prosecutor have officially acknowledged it. While many factors explain this refusal, the high domestic political cost ranks as the most relevant. Human rights groups insist that the state's attitude means victims may go unattended, while NGOs are obliged to set up ad hoc protection mechanisms. Some government officials also regret the lack of official recognition of this issue, but at the same time claim ongoing police efforts to pre[…]ime is not appreciated either.

III.Deportation and Gangs: The Spillover of … ecurity

U.S. migration policies in the 1990s exacted a heavy toll on El Salvador. Between 1998 and 2014, U.S. authorities deported almost 300,000 immigrants with criminal records to Central America. In El Salvador specifically, deportations between 1996 and 2002 led to the return of thousands of Salvadoran gang members who had fled their homeland during the war. Although U.S. policies sought to curb criminal activity by breaking up Los Angeles gangs, the long-term effect was an increase in violence across Central America and particularly El Salvador. When U.S. deportation figures and homicide data from El Salvador police are compiled, the rise in killings that followed mass criminal deportations stands out, especially in areas with higher gang presence. This strong correlation between U.S. deportations and homicide rates in the receiving country suggests some sort of causal link between the two (see figure 2 for the trend lines in murder rates and criminal deportations).

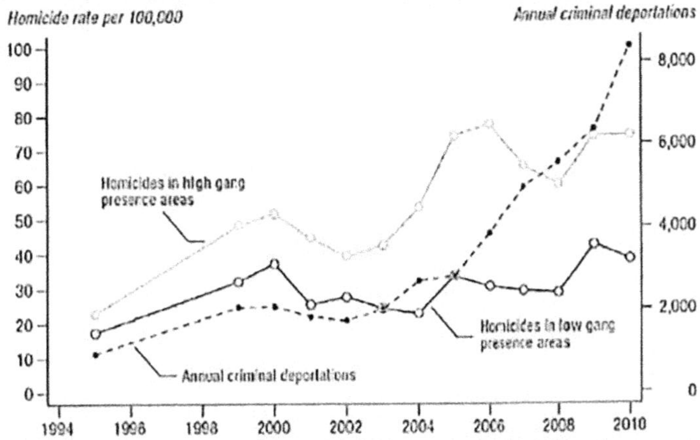

Figure 2. Homicide rates in municipalities with low and high gang presence and yearly criminal deportations from the U.S. National Civilian Police and U.S. Department of Homeland Security.

Salvadoran authorities now fear a fresh wave of mass deportations. Initial action and rhetoric indicates that U.S. President Trump's administration does not regard Central American migration so much as a flight from insecurity but rather as a conduit for greater violence in the U.S. Migration control and tough measures against gangs, above all the MS-13, have become matters of paramount importance. Indeed, Salvadoran gangs have received unprecedented attention from top-level U.S. officials, including a visit by Attorney General Jeff Sessions to El Salvador in late July. Tellingly, in the first months of Trump's mandate, undocumented migrant detentions increased 38 per cent while the administration began winding down protection schemes for minors such as the Central American Minors (CAM) and the Deferred Action for Child Arrivals (DACA).

The most critical decision for El Salvador is now the prospective termination in March 2018 of the Temporary Protected Status (TPS) for 195,000 of its nationals living in the U.S., none of whom can be considered criminals since they have registered and reported regularly to U.S. authorities for more than fifteen years, and have not been found to have violated national laws. More than 80 per cent are employed. Yet according to the U.S. State Department, Central Americans "no longer need to be shielded from deportation".

The renegotiation of the North American Free Trade Agreement (NAFTA) and El Salvador's close ties to Venezuela have complicated the country's search for regional allies as it faces a hostile U.S. administration. Along with its Northern Triangle neighbours, El Salvador has become a Mexican bargaining chip in the NAFTA talks, as Mexico seeks to gain Washington's sympathy and support by stressing its role as a buffer state able to both control undocumented migration along its southern border and foster economic development in Central America. The FMLN's relations with Venezuela's ruling party, the United Socialist Party of Venezuela (PSUV), also have lumped El Salvador together with the small number of Latin American countries still supportive of Caracas.

IV.The Evolution of Security Policies

Law enforcement campaigns based on mass captures and joint operations by police and the armed forces are common denominators of anti-gang policies over the last fifteen years. However, the gangs' rapid evolution has outpaced the rigid policy approaches developed in response.

A.Mano Dura

Between 1992 and 1999, the ARENA governments of Alfredo Cristiani and Armando Calderón Sol sought to consolidate the peace accords. With UN support, they undertook landmark security reforms, such as creation of a new civilian police force, separation of the intelligence service from the military, establishment of a human rights prosecutor and major changes to the armed forces' mandate and size. These swift transformations, along with a sudden peak in postwar violence, hindered the state's response to record criminal violence in the early 1990s, with 131 killings per 100,000 habitants in 1994.

After a steady fall in homicides in the ensuing years, U.S. deportations appear to have contributed to rapid gang expansion in the late 1990s. President Francisco Flores (1999-2004), also from ARENA, launched the first anti-gang plans in El Salvador in 2003, through the "Iron Fist Plan" (Plan Mano Dura) and Anti-gang Bill. Both plans were announced eight months before the 2004 presidential election, suggesting to many observers that they were in essence electorally-driven strategies. The "Iron Fist Plan" was launched in October 2003, and included joint operations by the police and the military known as "anti-gang task forces". The Anti-gang Bill, approved in December 2003, provided a temporary legal framework for the plan, criminalising gang membership and allowing detention of underage suspects.

ARENA again won the elections in 2004, and President Antonio Saca (2004-2009) launched the "Super Iron Fist Plan" (Plan Súper Mano Dura), continuing his predecessor's approach while incorporating prevention and rehabilitation plans. His two initiatives – "Helping Hand" (Mano Amiga) and "Extended Hand" (Mano Extendida) – identified priority communities and targeted at-risk youth and jailed gang members with special programs. However, lack of investment, delays in implementation and the low number of participants minimised their impact.

A continuous rise in violence led President Saca to relaunch his anti-gang efforts with a focus on strengthening police presence in violent hotspots and dismantling extortion rackets, an important source of gang income by that time. But the large number of captures – 30,934 in two years – did not result in more convictions. Around 84 per cent of those detained were released by Salvadoran judges due to flimsy evidence of gang affiliation, as well as legal inconsistencies between the recently created anti-gang laws and existing legislation on minors.

B.The Truce

Former TV anchor and FMLN standard bearer Mauricio Funes won the presidential election in 2009 and kick-started parallel prevention and repressive anti-crime campaigns. Funes government launched the first national violence prevention strategies between 2010 and 2013, which aimed to reduce the effects of criminal activity through actions targeted at the general public, people at risk and convicts. The strategies nevertheless proved to be little more than declarations of good intentions. The Funes administration simultaneously intensified joint police and military operations and approved the Gang Proscription Law in September 2010.

With the number of killings again reaching historic highs – 4,354 people were murdered in 2011 – Funes and his security cabinet changed tack, initiating an indirect dialogue with gang leaders to reduce killings in excha[illegible] better conditions in jails. The process, known as the "gang truce", was in [illegible]e a ceasefire agreement between the largest gangs starting in March 2012 after th[illegible]nment transferred some of their leaders from maximum security prisons t[illegible] strictive facilities. General Munguía Payés, who was then minister of justice and p[illegible] security and one of the strongest supporters of the process, appointed Fat[illegible]andres, head of the military bishopric, and former FMLN combatant Raúl Mijango as mediators, leading to frequent meetings with gang members and a drastic decrease in homicide rates.

However, lack of broad public and political support contributed to the end of the de facto truce. The FMLN and ARENA distanced themselves from negotiations, and were sceptical as to their impact on homicides, as were a majority of Salvadorans. Not even President Funes publicly admitted that the truce was official state policy. The truce started to collapse in 2013 after the Supreme Court declared that it was unconstitutional for a military officer to be in charge of the civilian police force, and Munguía Payés returned to his former post as defence minister. His successor, Ricardo Perdomo, declared in his first week in office that the government was not engaged in dialogue with the gangs. By the end of this process, in the second half of 2013, killings skyrocketed again, while gang extortion and recruitment, which had remained stable during the truce, increased afterwards.

C.New Measures

Sánchez Cerén, also from the FMLN, narrowly won the presidency in 2014 and the onset of his tenure was marked by deteriorating security. In early 2015, his administration launched joint military and police rapid-reaction forces and approved so-called "extraordinary measures" in March 2016. The government has also sought to target gang finances under the aegis of 'Operation Jaque' in July 2017 and 'Operación Tecana' in September 2017.

Although the focus of Sánchez Cerén's security policies has been law enforcement, violence prevention initiatives also made some headway under the 'Safe El Salvador' plan. Implementation came in various phases, starting in municipalities affected by higher levels of violence. Costing around $200 million per year, the plan is financed by international cooperation funds and an earmarked tax approved in November 2015. Of the $93 million collected in 2017 from these special taxes, around 70 per cent went to financing the police and the armed forces.

The merits of the new strategy have been disputed, as have its alleged accompanying human rights violations in the last two years. Total homicides fell by 20 per cent from 2015 to 2016, and government officials had estimated another 27 per cent drop by the end of 2017. However, this foreseen reduction has not been sustained, nor has the general public noted a significant fall in violence. The second half of 2017 witnessed an uptick in violence, including 687 murders between September and October 2017. In a stunning admission, a senior government official said that authorities were "fighting a war that cannot be won".

V.Critical Flaws in Security Policies

For the past fifteen years, El Salvador's security policies have struggled to contain the gang problem, which puts enormous pressure on the country's institutions. Lack of adequate investment or qualified personnel has undermined prevention initiatives, putting the onus on more aggressive forms of policing. Residents in gang-controlled areas – especially women and children – pay the highest price as a result of the current escalation of violence.

A.Public Policies and Institutional Weakness

The National Civil Police, which spearheads implementation of anti-gang policies, has been profoundly affected both by the tide of gang violence and by the policies chosen to respond to it. Officers argue that the police has become the favoured institution to lead the fight against crime, but that it cannot fulfil its role without support from other government institutions. The state response to the rise of targeted killings and armed confrontations with gangs in recent years has focused on small increases in wages, while much-needed support to families of deceased officers and permanent protection mechanisms have been absent, mostly due to financial constraints rather than a lack of political will. Allegations of abuse by the police have also received limited attention. Although the police has a relatively efficient internal control unit, it lacks the personnel required to process the growing number of allegations against officers.

In the context of generic institutional weakness, the armed forces, which continue to count on broad public support, remain the favoured option to combat gang violence. However, military support to police efforts has expanded without a legal framework determining the military's specific role in public security. According to the Salvadoran constitution, its role is strictly circumscribed to foreign threats, reflecting the demilitarisation of public security that was one of the pillars of the peace accords. The use of executive decrees over the last decade to normalise its role has put this institution into a legal limbo.

Judicial efforts to prosecute suspected criminals are constrained by the lack of a solid body of legislation to combat gang violence and of forensic evidence to try culprits. The Anti-gang Bill (2003) and its 2004 successor included a broad range of features that could be used to determine membership in an "illicit association". In the following years prosecutors and police applied the law by rounding up 30,934 suspected gang members, but the courts only sent to prison around 15 per cent of those captured. Recent legislation has not changed this trend: according to one judge on the criminal circuit, evidence presented in court is still often highly circumstantial.

B.Violence Prevention and Its Limits

As illustrated by data on El Salvador's public spending on security, comparatively little is invested in prevention. From 2008 to 2014, the annual budget for justice and security rose by $120.2 million annually, to reach $775 million a year, equivalent to about 3 per cent of annual GDP in 2014. Some 44 per cent of the 2011 security budget was invested in the police and justice ministry, 31 per cent in the judiciary, and only 1 per cent on prevention. The current allocation of funds is similar: though the government has committed to investing over two thirds of the special security taxes on prevention, in reality it allocates less than 40 per cent.

Whereas all recent governments have admitted the need for a holistic approach to combating gang violence and its root causes, preventive strategies have tended to feature more on paper than in practice. El Salvador's highly competitive two-party system steers policymakers toward measures that are politically and electorally appealing rather than those that address the multiple causes behind the gang phenomenon. Public fatigue, chronic violence and demands for punishment favour such coercive approaches. An FMLN security adviser identified the lack of political will and public outrage as the main difficulties in promoting alternative security measures: "people fall in love with repression".

Security officials maintain that prevention plans "are the most important" aspects of anti-crime policy but fear they cannot produce quick, tangible results. They also are concerned that these results cannot easily translate into either electoral support or attract sustainable funding. In this respect, the challenges faced by the Salvadoran government are not unique and affect other Latin American countries confronting high levels of violent crime. Authorities tend to avoid the political risks and uncertainties of combating criminality and its root causes by handing the security forces discretionary power to tackle the problem.

In the context of chronic insecurity, crime experts likewise question whether violence prevention initiatives can have a notable impact. The head of a NGO said: "the [social] disintegration [in El Salvador] is such that [prevention] programs are not sufficient … [decision makers] look away when you explain to them that this repression-prevention duality does not work". Both ARENA and FMLN members referred to the ways ongoing repressive measures undermine alternative policies, with some arguing that "in this context, it [prevention] doesn't work".

Lukewarm support for prevention initiatives and resort to traditional coercive policing methods also explain the limited impact until now of the 'Safe El Salvador' plan. Although it is true that prioritised municipalities have seen a reduction in homicides of up to 60 per cent, statistically murder rates in the plan's target municipalities have remained quite similar to those in other locations since December 2015, when the plan was first launched. This is illustrated in Figure 3 below, which shows similar patterns both in prioritised municipalities under the 'Safe El Salvador' plan and non-prioritised municipalities.

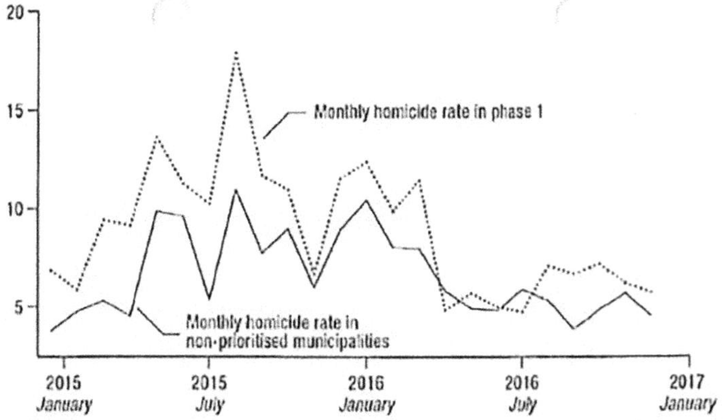

Figure 3. Homicides rates in municipalities prioritised by Plan Safe El Salvador versus homicide rates in non-prioritised municipalities. National Civilian Police and U.S. Department of Homeland Security

C.Lack of Employment Opportunities and Increasing Poverty

El Salvador's sluggish economic performance and worsening fiscal conditions have impeded job creation for young men hailing from marginalised areas. According to the IMF, the country's growth – on average 1.9 per cent between 2010 and 2016 – was one of the slowest in the Central American region, a reality it attributed to "crime, outward migration, consumption bias, and low savings". The current budget deficit stands at around 3 per cent of GDP, and public debt is expected to reach 61 per cent of GDP by the end of 2017. Some 25 per cent of Salvadorans aged fifteen-24 are neither working nor studying.

Although unemployed youth are more vulnerable to gang recruitment there are few public policies aimed at promoting training and generating employment for young people. According to the 2017 Florida International University study, only 35 per cent of gang members interviewed have ever received professional training. Of those that did, nearly 70 per cent were trained in manual work. Gang members' aspirations, however, are considerably higher, with over 40 per cent wishing to join a profession or become an entrepreneur.

El Salvador also suffers persistently high poverty rates that increased between 2014 and 2015, mostly in urban areas. This has made implementation of prevention programs even harder, since officials tend to find that demands expressed by residents in marginalised communities are geared more to basic needs or food than improved public spaces or enhanced community facilities. "I arrived in a prioritised community where I went to give a talk on peacebuilding, and I realised how far from reality we were when people told me they didn't even have drinking water", explained an official from San Miguel municipality in charge of implementing "Safe El Salvador".

D.El Salvador's Social Fabric: The Unaddressed Root Causes

The most important flaw in security policies is their failure to address living conditions in gang-controlled communities. Social anomie, the victimisation of youth and women and a climate of constant fear and suspicion help explain both the resilience of gangs and how well-intentioned policies fail to affect realities on the ground.

1.Gang control and community bonds

There is a consensus among the highest security authorities in El Salvador on the need to reestablish state territorial control as the prelude to improving security. In some areas, gangs have accumulated so much power that they have become de facto custodians of these localities, setting up road blocks, supervising everyday life and imposing their own law. "Gangs did not steal the territory from the state, they simply occupied it when it was empty [after the armed conflict]", explained one NGO worker.

At the same time, vigilante activity has become a common threat, especially in areas with major gang presence. These patrols are formed by civilians, some of them war veterans, who seek to stop the entrance of gang members in their territory. No public policy of the past fifteen years has sought to restrict these groups, or reduce their potential harm. Vigilantism has even been promoted by lawmakers such as the President of the Legislative Assembly Guillermo Gallegos, who has admitted financing some of these groups. Gruesome pictures of slain alleged criminals appear regularly in social media accounts attributed to these groups, whose followers "celebrate the elimination of gang members".

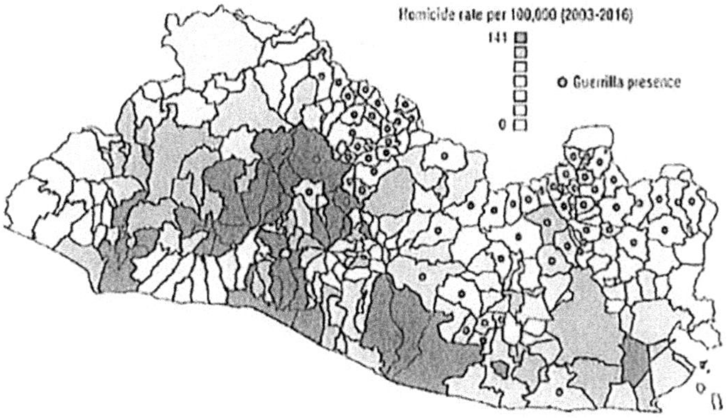

Figure 4. Guerrilla presence in 1982 and average homicide rates 2003-2016 El Salvador National Civil Police; historical map from Cornell University PJ Mode "Collection of Persuasive Cartography" indicating the areas of control by FMLN guerrilla in 1982

In general, areas with strong social and community bonds have seen far less gang expansion. While there are no empirical studies decisively proving this link, the map in

Figure 4 suggests a significant correlation. Ta[illegible] strength of the insurgency during the civil war as a proxy for social cohe[illegible]ce guerrillas depended on strong communal ties and collective mobilisation). W[illegible] shows that in 2015 districts where the insurgency had been strong had re[illegible] few homicides in comparison with districts where the insurgency was weak.

Previous studies have pointed to how a lack of community ties underpinned the expansion of gang control in parts of Central America, and how the presence of these groups proceeded to further undermine social cohesion. Whereas organised communities have been able to limit the impact of gang violence in their municipalities, a 2007 survey from across the Northern Triangle found that 68 per cent of Salvadorans interviewed in gang-affected areas reported that they did not collaborate with their neighbours in dealing with crime problems in their community. The survey showed that interviewees in El Salvador and other regional countries instead had opted to change their daily habits, such as avoiding walking alone after sunset or buying a gun. Some individuals who lived in gang controlled areas also mentioned the limits on free movement imposed by these groups as a crucial factor behind the deterioration of community life.

2.The victims: women, children and teenagers

Young people are prime victims of the country's insecurity, targeted by state law enforcement on one side and gangs on the other. The first "iron fist" plans in 2003-2004 targeted youth suspected of criminal activity, despite warnings from the UN Committee on the Rights of the Child that these new rules were too harsh on minors.
Lack of investment in education coupled with criminal activity in and around schools allows gangs to use them as recruitment platforms. Tellingly, spending on education in El Salvador is the lowest in Central America, representing only 4.4 per cent of GDP. Many schools are unsafe for students and teachers, both of whom are threatened by gang members and their children. A 2015 report from El Salvador's Ministry of Education estimated that about 65 per cent of schools are affected by gangs. In these schools, almost 30 per cent of staff have reported threats.

The effect of gang recruitment and presence on education can be illustrated by comparing years of schooling in areas with a high gang presence to those with a low gang presence. Figure 5 shows that individuals who started school in 1990 and lived in what are now high-gang presence areas had significantly more years of schooling than their peers in areas that now boast a low gang presence, largely because education is weaker in rural areas, which tend to have fewer gangs. The schooling gap was reduced by nearly half over the next six years, mainly because of improvements in rural education. But much more strikingly, the gap was erased completely over the next six years between 1996 and 2002, not because of further improvements in rural education (indeed, years of schooling in rural locations declined slightly over that time) but rather because of the precipitous drop in schooling in high-gang areas. That drop can be explained by the mass deportation to El Salvador beginning in 1996, which had a highly detrimental effect on schooling.

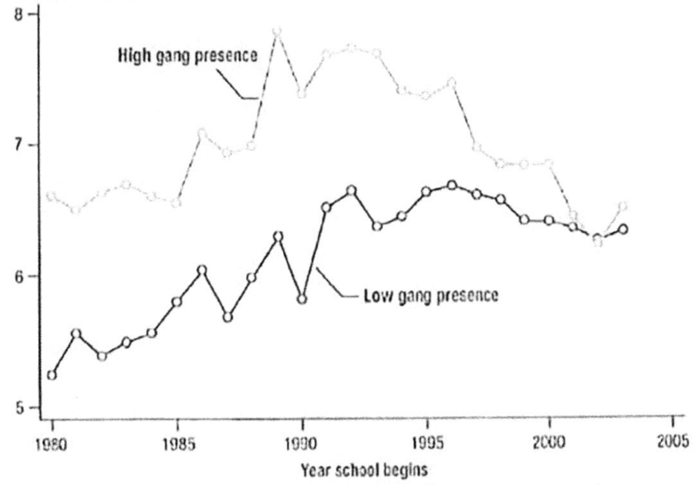

Figure 5: Average years of education in municipalities with low and high gang presence by the year school began Household surveys from 2012 and 2013. El Salvador General Directorate of Statistics and Census (DIGESTYC)

Women, meanwhile, are the forgotten victims of the country's security policies. Specific action to tackle the victimisation of women as civilians or as gang members has been missing from security policies. The role of women in the design and implementation of security policies is also limited, with no female members in El Salvador's security cabinet. The levels of violence against women make this absence from key decision-making circles all the more worrying. A total of 10,545 female minors were reported to have been raped between 2006 and 2014, amounting to one of the highest such rates in the hemisphere. Many more go unreported for fear of retaliation.

3."We fear each other": accounts from gang-controlled areas

Testimony from people living in gang-controlled communities reveal high levels of distrust of public authorities, limited access to public spaces, and physical abuse against young people. Below are some of the most representative and disturbing concerns voiced by interviewees, all young people between fourteen and 25 years old from the suburbs of San Salvador. The statements underline the difficulties in devising and applying effective security policies in a context of widespread control by gangs coupled with public animosity toward them.

VI.Opportunities Ahead

Conversations with high-level authorities suggest they are fully conscious of the limits of the repressive approach and the impossible task of prosecuting 500,000 alleged members of the gangs' support base. At the same time, the current government strategy aims at using all resources available to asphyxiate the gangs, including the militarisation of public spaces, to which the gangs have responded with greater violence. While there is little evidence to suggest that the government or opposition will soon offer distinct policies, actions such as adapting the current security strategy, promoting rehabilitation efforts and reinforcing security and justice institutions could contribute to reducing insecurity.

A."Safe El Salvador" and Territorial Recovery

Avoiding past mistakes and maintaining political support for government initiatives at the local level are some of the main principles behind the "Safe El Salvador" plan. Although there are doubts as to the plan's achievements on the first score, the local approach of the plan has become a powerful tool for the main parties to bolster their electoral bases in municipalities they control. Large sums of money have been poured into the prioritised locations and allowed mayors to offer visible changes to communities.

Converting "Safe El Salvador" into an effective territorial recovery strategy will require more intensive efforts to support at-risk populations. Since young people are both the primary victims and perpetrators of gang violence, it is essential to ensure that schools remain safe havens.

The changing dynamics of criminal violence i[illegible]vador also suggest the need for a differentiated security strategy for areas [illegible]gh and low gang presence. The "Safe El Salvador" plan could be continued for the most affected municipalities, while areas with lower levels of violence could experime[illegible]h an alternative approach based on community policing, support for civil society and primary prevention aimed at limiting the appeal and power of gangs. In contrast, the current mass arrests and generic targeting of teenage suspects are detrimental to efforts to win local support and garner information. This was confirmed by a police officer in San Miguel, who acknowledged the importance of community support: "We can have thousands of agents, but if the community does not trust us, we cannot do anything".

Supporting this shift in policy will require fresh allocations of resources and a change in the partisan political habits. All political parties, and above all ARENA, should avoid blocking legislation on issues where there is in theory broad cross-party agreement. If ARENA's priority is winning the 2019 presidential elections, it should consider that a continued deterioration in security conditions could undermine support for the two-party system as a whole.

Although the government is clear that it has no intention to engage again in dialogue with gangs, in practice thousands of low-level officials and community leaders are compelled to negotiate daily with them. In private, political parties recognised de facto gangs' territorial presence all over the country. It is uncertain whether the gangs' offer to disband in January 2017 is still in place, but the government should keep the door open to grassroots non-violent approaches through support for the work of local churches and civil society, and avoid demonising those who are trying to reduce local violence. The chances of a fresh attempt at national dialogue with the gangs of the sort that failed between 2012 and 2013 would very much depend on the incoming administration in 2019.

B.Improving Judicial and Police Institutions

Legal reforms are urgently needed to relieve the judiciary of the pressures it faces. Possibilities include reducing sentences for minor offenses such as drug possession, or using trained community mediators to settle disputes outside of the courtroom, which has proven successful in Honduras. It is clear from interviews with judges and high-level magistrates that the distribution of judicial resources across the country is seriously imbalanced given the geographic clustering of criminal activity.
The prosecutor's office lacks the financial and human resources required to take on additional cases or swiftly process current ones. Ideally, it should receive more funding and revise its annual goals to ensure they are realistic. Alleged corruption scandals affecting the institution's previous leadership also underline the need to reinforce transparent and open selection procedures for high-level officials.

Lessons from police reforms in countries such as Guatemala and Honduras indicate that specific innovations can prove more effective than efforts to reform the entire security system. Better coordination between the police, the prosecutor's office and the courts stands out as one crucial area. The implementation of Guatemala's 2010 law against organised crime – allowing prosecutors working with investigative police to ask judges for permission to use wire taps – is an example of successful inter-agency coordination. The establishment of innovative systems of case management in the homicide investigations unit, which worked directly with prosecutors, has been fundamental to Guatemala's success in reducing murder rates in certain areas.

At the same time, the strengthening of the police internal affairs unit through additional personnel and resources could enhance the institution's transparency at a time of increasing concern over alleged abuses of power.

C.A State-led Rehabilitation Process

The most significant government effort in rehabilitating convicted criminals is the "I'm Changing" (Yo Cambio) program, which seeks to spur inmates into training each other in specific skills that fellow prisoners can offer. Despite a lack of resources, authorities argue it has had beneficial effects in jails such as Apanteo, Ilopango or San Vicente. At the same time, a handful of Salvadoran churches and business leaders are carrying out independent rehabilitation programs. The private sector's initiatives depend on the leadership of specific individuals, such as the well-known case of former gang members working for the sportswear company American League. Such programs help former gang members overcome the social stigma that can make it so hard for them to find a job or carry on a normal life.

More rehabilitation opportunities should be provided. The Legislative Assembly could debate and approve a bill initially presented to the Legislative Assembly Security Committee in early 2017 that has been stuck in Congress since then. This could be amended to incorporate lessons from the "I'm Changing" program and other rehabilitation initiatives provided by churches, NGOs and the private sector, and thus help the government develop one of the more neglected pillars of the "Safe El Salvador" plan. Specific measures should include financing tattoo removal, and developing a methodology for rehabilitation that protects participants from prosecution or offers reduced sentences. Rehabilitation measures could help prepare officials for an eventual handover of arms by some gang members, should this ever happen. As one government official explained: "If they [gangs] one day decide to surrender, we are screwed".

The construction of several new prisons is an important step toward reducing overcrowding, but should be accompanied by more and better trained prison personnel. Providing human rights training for guards is especially important.

D.Coordinating Efforts to Protect El Salvador from U.S. Migration Policies

El Salvador's security crisis, as well as its past vulnerability to U.S. migration policies, fully justifies continuing the Temporary Protected Status (TPS) designation that has allowed around 195,000 Salvadoran nationals to stay in the U.S. legally. While El Salvador was originally designated for this program after two earthquakes in 2001, the U.S. administration should also consider current circumstances, especially the humanitarian impact of criminal violence. The Department of Homeland Security's decision to end the program for Sudan, Nicaragua and Haiti suggests, however, that it will also choose to terminate TPS for El Salvador.

The high levels of violence in El Salvador make the country especially dangerous for returning migrants, especially for the 192,700 children of Salvadorans with TPS, many of whom are U.S. citizens. To mitigate the impact of TPS termination, the U.S. government should confirm its decision on the issue as early as possible, and preferably provide a long extension before the cut-off date. This would help El Salvador prepare accordingly for the arrival of the first wave, and give its affected nationals some predictability as to their future. Coordination between San Salvador and different consulates in the U.S. will be key to offering potential returnees dignified employment opportunities in their home country. In the best-case scenario, this would allow the country to develop job placement schemes in coordination with the private sector. Spanish education for the children of returnees, many of whom will speak English as their first language, should also be funded by the U.S.

Regardless of the TPS outcome, Salvadoran authorities should work with the main political parties to create and implement a policy for returnees. By the end of 2018, state institutions will need a plan to address the reception of returnees and the humanitarian risks faced by those wishing to migrate back to the U.S. Both the assembly and the incoming government – to be elected in early 2019 – should continue these efforts by intensifying locally-targeted policies to promote development and entrepreneurship in the municipalities that receive more returnees. This mid-term policy should have a strong educational focus, as the most vulnerable groups will be children between fourteen and eighteen years old who are easy prey for potential gang recruitment.

The Salvadoran government also needs to acknowledge the reality of internal displacement – which affects all Northern Triangle countries – and start to work on a humanitarian response in coordination with international agencies. This should include the adoption of the Comprehensive Regional Framework for the Protection and Solution (MIRPS), signed on 26 October 2017 by Mexico and all Central American countries, except El Salvador. The priority should be to offer temporary shelter and support to victims who cannot go back to their communities, most of them vulnerable groups such as children and women. The government could work in coordination with NGOs already handling some cases, learn from their experience, and create a screening system based on information previously gathered by these organisations.

VII.Conclusion

El Salvador's security crisis is a warning for Latin America and the world as to how the unexpected outcomes of a failed post-conflict transition can become more lethal than the war itself. A quarter of a century after the signing of its peace accords, El Salvador is often said to be suffering a "new war" between the state and gangs. However, this "war" is really a manifestation of social breakdown: the sides that are fighting one another are far from cohesive, gang violence has as yet no clear political objective, and the civilians most affected by insecurity, largely young people from low-income backgrounds, are both victims and perpetrators.

For the past fifteen years, the gangs have learned to shield themselves from different state security policies by transforming their operations and internal organisation. The current sophistication of these groups, as well as the repeated failure to address their socio-economic roots – roots which are themselves deepened and perpetuated by ongoing violence – is a sign that many of these policies, even including those aiming at prevention rather than repression, will need to be reformed and enhanced if they are to halt El Salvador's bloodshed.

However, under the umbrella of the "Safe El Salvador" plan, the government now has the opportunity to launch concerted rehabilitation programs and take advantage of the seemingly high number of gang members willing to leave criminal life. Cross-party agreements will be crucial in designing mechanisms to strengthen the prosecutor's office and the police, as well as for preparing integration mechanisms for mass deportations from the U.S. should Washington fail to redesignate the TPS program for resident Salvadorans. Minimising the risks of violence during the March 2018 local and legislative polls will likewise depend on the goodwill and cooperation of the two major parties. The fact that the FMLN and ARENA have been peacefully alternating in power for the last 25 years after an exceptionally brutal civil war is a sign that Salvadorans have the capacity to overcome hard times. The Salvadoran public and countries in the hemisphere will continue to voice outrage over the gangs' criminal deeds. But this violence is the latest manifestation, and probably not the last, of the country's long and painful history of social divides. Security policy that ignores these causes will do little to halt the carnage, and could well extend it for another generation

https://www.crisisgroup.org/latin-america-caribbean/central-america/el-salvador/64-el-salvadors-politics-perpetual-violence?utm_source=Sign+Up+to+Crisis+Group%27s+Email+Updates&utm_campaign=13c05cfd1c-EMAIL_CAMPAIGN_2017_12_19&utm_medium=email&utm_term=0_1dab8c11ea-13c05cfd1c-359000997

Follow Genocide Watch for more updates:

Like 0

Share this post:

THE ALLIANCE AGAINST GENOCIDE

ACT for SUDAN | AEGIS PREVENTING CRIMES AGAINST HUMANITY | ANTIQUITIES COALITION | ANUAK JUSTICE COUNCIL

Genocide Watch is the Coordinator of the Alliance Against Genocide. Founded in 1999, the Alliance is made up of over 75 organizations from around the world and was the first coalition of organizations focused completely on preventing genocide.

Webmaster Login

EXHIBIT '22':
It's so Dangerous to Police MS-13 in El Salvador that Officers are Fleeing the Country – The Washington Post – 03/03/2019

The Washington Post

The Americas

It's so dangerous to police MS-13 in El Salvador that officers are fleeing the country

By Kevin Sieff
March 3

SAN SALVADOR — They were given one of the most dangerous tasks in policing: Take down MS-13.

They were bankrolled by the United States and trained by FBI agents. But members of the Salvadoran police have been killed by the dozens in each of the past three years, most in attacks that investigators and experts blame on MS-13, an international street gang. At least nine officers were killed in the first month of this year.

Now, a number of El Salvador's police officers are fleeing the gang they were tasked with eliminating.

There is no list in either El Salvador or the United States of Salvadoran police officers who have fled the country. But The Washington Post has identified 15 officers in the process of being resettled as refugees by the United Nations and six officers who have either recently received asylum or have scheduled asylum hearings in U.S. immigration courts. In WhatsApp groups, police officers have begun discussing the possibility of a migrant caravan composed entirely of Salvadoran police — a *caravana policial*, the officers call it.

The exodus of Salvadoran police points to how the country's security forces have failed to break the stranglehold of organized crime. It also shows that among those seeking refuge in the United States during the Trump administration are some of America's closest security partners.

"These are among the most vulnerable people in El Salvador," said Julio Buendía, the director of migration at Cáritas El Salvador, a nonprofit organization that works with the United States and United Nations on refugee resettlement.

The United States has been bolstering the Salvadoran police, part of a regional strategy intended to stabilize Central America's most violent countries and reduce migration. The State Department spent at least $48 million to train police in El Salvador, Guatemala and Honduras from 2014 through 2017, according to the Government Accountability Office.

The department opened a law enforcement training academy in San Salvador, where 855 Salvadoran officers were trained by the FBI and other American law enforcement agencies in those four years.

"The Salvadoran government, with U.S. government support, has made significant gains in the area of security, including reductions in homicides and every other category of violent crime measured," the State Department said in a statement issued in response to an inquiry by The Post.

Citing "privacy reasons," the department would not comment on whether it was receiving asylum or refugee applications from Salvadoran police officers.

By some measures, the U.S.-backed security efforts appeared to be showing results. In 2018, El

Salvador's murder rate was 50.[illegible] per 100,000 inhabitants. That was s[illegible] among the highest in the world, but it was down from 60.8 per 100,000 in 2017 and 81 per 100,000 in 2016.

MS-13 was born in Los Angeles in the late 1970s, expanding as more Salvadorans arrived in the United States after fleeing the country's civil war. The group splintered, with Barrio 18 becoming a chief rival, and both groups grew in American prisons before reaching El Salvador through mass deportations. Between 2001 and 2010, the United States deported 40,429 ex-convicts to El Salvador, according to the Department of Homeland Security.

El Salvador's government adopted an "iron fist" response to the gangs, including more police operations. When that approach failed, it tried to broach a truce with the gangs in 2014. The pact quickly disintegrated and was followed by another surge in violence. It was then that the gangs began to explicitly broadcast their threats against police officers.

"If you kill a 'pig,' or a police officer, you're more respected in these gangs. That's the policy — using death as exchange currency," said Héctor Silva Ávalos, a journalist and researcher who has written a book on the Salvadoran police and has served as an expert witness at several asylum hearings for former police officers in the United States.

With salaries of $300 to $400 per month, the low-level police officers who make up the majority of the force often have no choice but to live in neighborhoods vulnerable to gangs. And so, in the vast majority of the cases, police officers are killed when they are home from work or are on leave.

In August, Manuel de Jesús Mira Díaz was killed while buying construction materials. In July, Juan de Jesús Morales Alvarado was killed while walking with his 7-year-old son on the way to school. In November, Barrera Mayén was killed after taking leave to spend time at home with his family.

The police investigated a number of the killings since 2014 and found members of the major gangs responsible.

"They have more control than we do. When we go home, we're in neighborhoods where there's one police to 100 gang members. We're easy victims," said one officer in the country's anti-gang unit, who, after being threatened by MS-13 in his home, is awaiting refugee status from the United Nations. He spoke on the condition of anonymity out of fear for his safety.

Complicating their response to the threats, Salvadoran police are also not legally allowed to take their weapons home with them.

"I bring it home anyway. I sleep with it on my waist," said a female officer, who is awaiting refugee status from the United Nations and spoke on the condition of anonymity out of fear for her safety. "My husband and I take turns sleeping. We know they are going to come for us."

Many units in the Salvadoran police are forbidden to wear balaclavas to conceal their identities. In anti-gang units, officers are allowed to wear such masks during operations, but they are frequently asked to testify in court, where they must show their faces and identify themselves by name while gang members look on.

In 2017, El Salvador's attorney general, Douglas Meléndez, urged the government to do more to protect off-duty police, asking the parliament to pass a "protection law" for police and soldiers that would also provide funding to protect their families. The law was never passed.

Last month, security concerns played a central role in a presidential election won by San Salvador's 37-year-old former mayor, Nayib Bukele. At least 285 people were killed in January, leading up to the vote, which many saw as the gangs' attempt to leverage their influence amid the election campaign. In a security plan leaked to the Salvadoran news media, Bukele's campaign wrote: "The expansion of these criminal groups is undeniable, as is the impact on the lives of ordinary citizens."

In response to the targeting of police officers this year, El Salvador's police chief introduced a policy: For their own protection, officers were not allowed to return to their homes. The police chief declined multiple interview requests.

Many officers, feeling unprotected by their own force, have said their only option is to leave the country.

Organizations that work with the United Nations to resettle Salvadoran refugees in the United States say they have found more and more police officers arriving unannounced at their offices. In addition to the 21 asylum seekers and refugees identified by The Post, several others have recently arrived in Spain and Mexico, according to news reports, applying for humanitarian visas or other forms of protection. Lawyers for police officers and many officers themselves say that far more officers are preparing to flee.

One of the cases that Buendía, the migration director of Cáritas, referred to the United Nations High Commissioner for Refugees is an officer who survived two attacks while off duty. First, he was shot eight times by suspected gang members; then, two years later, he was shot four times. The officer pleaded for protection from his commander.

Buendía included a letter from the commander in the officer's refugee application. "There's nothing we can do for you," the commander wrote. "You need to protect yourself."

A police spokesman declined to comment on the letter.

In one case, concerning a police officer now applying for asylum in U.S. immigration courts, gang members threatened to kidnap the officer's child at an elementary school in rural El Salvador.

"That's not what these guys signed up for. It's one thing to be shot at on the job. It's another for your family to be targeted while you're off duty," said Emily Smith, the attorney representing the officer.

Lawyers such as Smith who are representing the officers typically try to explain to immigration judges that as former police officers, their clients would be persecuted if they were forced to return to El Salvador. But the attorneys are also aware of how narrowly U.S. asylum law can be applied, and that the courts are unlikely to grant asylum to all former officers.

"What we chose to do is focus on the specific threats facing our client," said Patrick Courtney, who last year represented a Salvadoran officer who had been physically assaulted in his home before fleeing. "We focused on his anti-gang views, on the fact that the threats were directed at him individually."

Courtney's client was granted asylum late last year. They discussed where he would live in the United States, and what he would do next. The former officer had only one goal: He wanted to join the United States military.

0 Comments

Kevin Sieff
Kevin Sieff has been The Washington Post's Latin America correspondent since 2018. He served previously as the paper's Africa bureau chief and Afghanistan bureau chief. Follow

---

EXHIBIT '23':
Events of 2018: El Salvador – Human Rights

El Salvador

Events of 2018

A man reads the names on a memorial monument during the 37th anniversary of El Mozote Massacre in the village of El Mozote, Meanguera, El Salvador, December 8, 2018.

Available In: **English** | Español

Government Accountability

Abuses by Security Forces

Prison Conditions

Gangs

Children's Rights

Women's Sexual and Reproductive Rights

LGBT Rights

Attacks on Journalists

Key International Actors

he world's highest homicide

Gangs continued in 2018 to exercise territorial control and extort residents in municipalities throughout the country. They forcibly recruit children and subject some women, girls, and lesbian, gay, bisexual, and transgender (LGBT) individuals to sexual slavery. Gangs kill, disappear, rape, or displace those who resist them, including government officials, security forces, and journalists.

Security forces have been largely ineffective in protecting the population from gang violence and have committed egregious abuses, including the extrajudicial execution of alleged gang members, sexual assaults, and enforced disappearances.

Girls and women alleged to have had abortions have been imprisoned for homicide and aggravated homicide, including during the year. LGBT individuals also face discrimination and violence. These conditions have resulted in internal and cross-border displacement.

Government Accountability

While impunity for government abuses and corruption continue to be the norm, in recent years, El Salvador has taken some steps to bring former officials to justice.

In July 2016, the Supreme Court declared unconstitutional a 1993 amnesty law that prohibited the prosecution of war crimes and crimes against humanity, committed overwhelmingly by state security forces, according to the United Nations Truth Commission, during the country's civil war (1979-1992). In March 2017, former military commanders were brought to trial for their alleged responsibility for the 1981 El Mozote massacre, in which 978 civilians died, including 553 children, and soldiers committed mass rapes. The trial was ongoing at time of writing.

Four other cases remained open but had not reached trial, including one related to the assassination of Archbishop Oscar Romero as he celebrated mass in a hospital chapel in March 1980, a day after his radio homily begging soldiers to stop their repression and killings. In October, a judge ordered the arrest of ex-Cpt. Alvaro Saravia for his alleged role in planning the crime.

In September, a court sentenced former President Antonio Saca and various members of his administration to 5-10 years in prison for embezzling more than US$301 million of public funds to enrich themselves and bribe officials and journalists during his presidency (2004-2009). The ruling followed the attorney general's arrest of 32 people in former President Mauricio Funes' (2009-2014) circle for allegedly embezzling $351 million through the same

You Should Be Worrying about the Woman Shortage

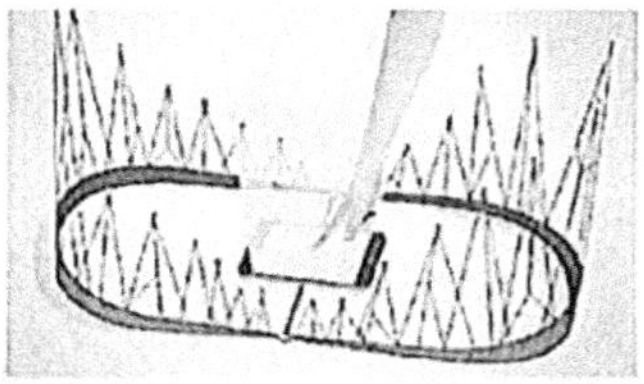

Social Media's Moral Reckoning
Changing the Terms of Engagement with Silicon Valley

As China's Grip Tightens, Global Institutions Gasp
Limiting Beijing's Influence Over Accountability and Justice

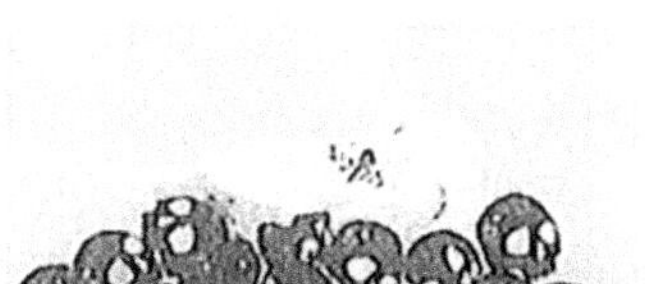

Atrocities as the New Normal
Time to Re-Energize the "Never

Again" Movement

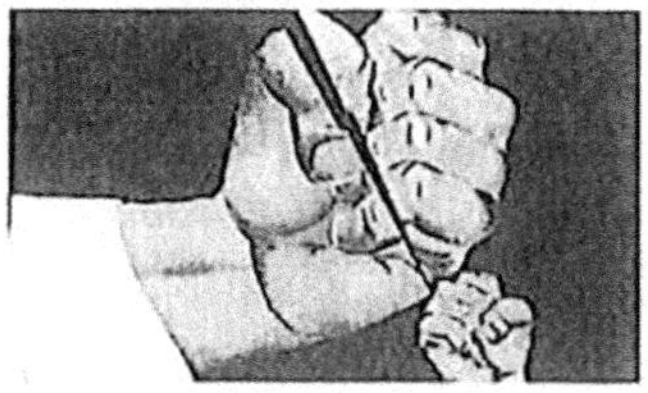

Caught in the Middle
Convincing "Middle Powers" to Fight Autocrats Despite High Costs

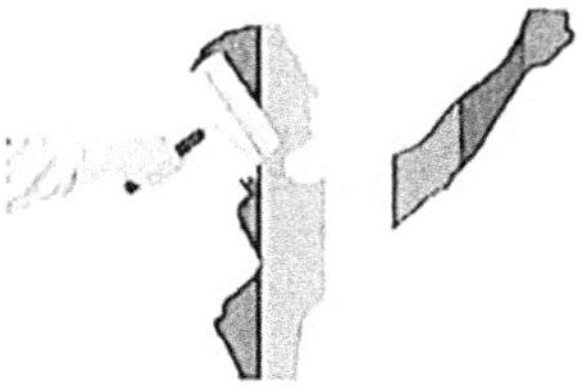

Breaking the Buzzword
Fighting the "Gender Ideology" Myth

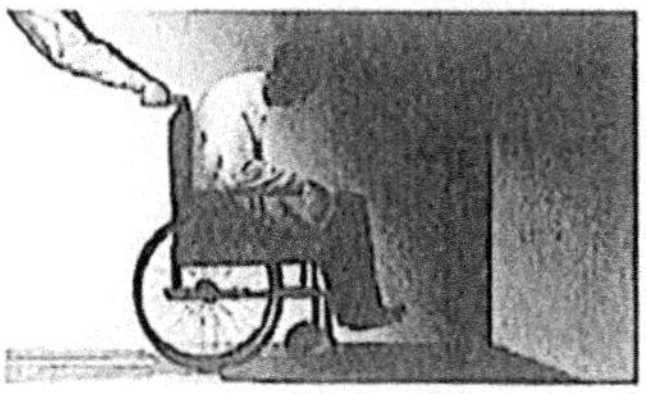

Living Longer, Locked Away
Helping Older People Stay Connected, and at Home

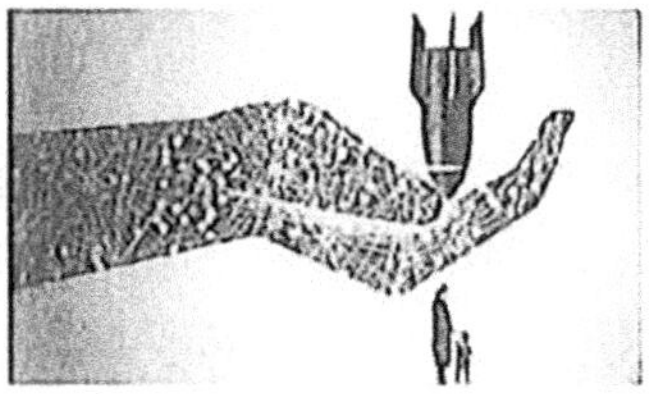

Can Algorithms Save Us from Human Error?
Human Judgment and Responsibility

mechanism. In January 2016, former President Francisco Flores (1999-2004) died while he was being investigated for similar crimes.

Abuses by Security Forces

Since taking office in 2014, President Salvador Sánchez Cerén has expanded the military's role in public security operations, despite a 1992 peace accord stipulation that it not be involved in policing. Killings of alleged gang members by security forces in supposed "armed confrontations" increased from 142 in 2013 to 591 in 2016. In her June 2018 report, the UN special rapporteur on extrajudicial killings found a "pattern of behavior ... amounting to extrajudicial executions and excessive use of force" by state security.

A 2017 investigative report in the Salvadoran online newspaper Revista Factum documented evidence of a "death squad" within an elite unit of the Salvadoran police that engaged in killings, sexual assault of teenage girls, robbery, and extortion. At the funeral of a female police officer in September, the National Civil Police (Policia Nacional Civil) director stated that another, now-defunct elite unit participated in her December 2017 disappearance and "femicide," which Salvadoran law defines as a killing motivated by hatred or contempt for women.

In their 2017 and 2018 visits, the UN special rapporteurs on internal displacement and extrajudicial killings documented threats and harassment by security forces against members of the LGBT population, individuals who work toward gang members' rehabilitation, and adolescent children and young adults.

Prison Conditions

In August, the Legislative Assembly made permanent a "state of emergency" that put inmates at seven prisons on lockdown and suspended their family visits. El Salvador first declared the emergency state in March 2016, then extended it as part of its "extraordinary measures" to combat crime in April 2016.

Designed to hold up to 11,400 inmates, the country's penal institutions held more than 38,700 in January. Approximately 30 percent are in pretrial or remand detention.

Cases of tuberculosis among inmates increased from 96 in March 2016 to 1,272 in January 2018. Access to visit prisons has been restricted, but international journalists allowed to enter have noted prisoners' skeletal appearance. More were killed or died in the prisons in 2018 than in 2017.

Gangs

According to widely reported figures, approximately 60,000 gang members are present in at least 247 of the country's 262 municipalities. They enforce their territories' borders and extort and gather intelligence on residents and those transiting these areas, particularly around public transport, schools, and markets.

Numerous security and elected officials have collaborated with gangs in criminal operations, according to international and national media. According to media reports, all political parties have negotiated with them for conducting campaigns, voting, and daily operations and on a truce begun in 2012 between national government, 11 municipal governments, and the two largest gangs.

In April 2016, the Legislative Assembly modified an existing counterterrorism statute to explicitly classify gangs as terrorist organizations and reformed its penal code to impose prison sentences of up to 15 years on anyone who "solicits, demands, offers, promotes, formulates, negotiates, convenes or enters into a non-persecution agreement" with gangs. The UN special rapporteur on extrajudicial killings noted a large discrepancy between charges for membership in a terrorist organization and convictions for it. The Attorney General's Office used the reforms to retroactively prosecute current and former officials who participated in truce negotiations from 2012 to 2014.

Children's Rights

Various local and international officials believe child abuse is widespread. In 2017, 46 girls and 311 boys were murdered, according to the Institute of Legal Medicine, and at least 20 girls and 14 boys were disappeared, according to the Attorney General's Office. Judges absolved rapists of children as young as 12, if they "formed a home" or had a child together.

In August 2017, the Legislative Assembly prohibited marriage below the age of 18 in all circumstances, ending an exception for pregnant girls.

Women's Sexual and Reproductive Rights

Since 1998, abortion is illegal under all circumstances. Providers and those who assist with the procedure face prison sentences of between six months and 12 years.

In 2018, the Legislative Assembly considered two proposals for modifications to the penal code to permit abortion in cases of rape, grave fetal malformations, or risks to the health of the mother. Support was insufficient to bring either to a vote.

More than 150 girls and women were prosecuted in the past two decades. The courts accepted as evidence a floating lung test that forensic pathologists deemed unreliable over a century ago.

At least 20 women remained imprisoned at time of writing on charges of manslaughter, homicide, or aggravated homicide for allegedly having abortions. In February, the Supreme Court determined there was not enough evidence to prove Teodora Vasquez harmed her fetus and released her 10 years into her 30-year sentence. In March, Maira Figueroa was released 15 years into her 30-year sentence, after the Supreme Court decided charges for aggravated homicide were "excessive and immoral," given that the then-19-year-old became pregnant from rape and had obstetric complications.

LGBT Rights

LGBT individuals are targets of homophobic and transphobic violence, including by police and gang members. Since 1994, over 600 have been killed, according to four Salvadoran LGBT rights organizations.

El Salvador introduced hate crimes into its penal code in September 2015. To date, no cases have been prosecuted as hate crimes. Human Rights Watch is not aware of any bias-related murders of known LGBT individuals that have resulted in conviction.

Attacks on Journalists

Journalists reporting on abuses of power or corruption at various outlets are targets of death threats, as are journalists living in gang-controlled neighborhoods.

In the past decade, at least seven journalists have been murdered. In three cases between 2011 and 2016, Salvadoran courts convicted gang members, who had targeted journalists because of their reporting.

Key International Actors

For fiscal year 2018, the United States disbursed over $42 million in bilateral aid to El Salvador.

In her April report, the UN special rapporteur for internal displacement noted a "striking disparity between government figures [in the hundreds] on those internally displaced by [State and gang] violence and those of civil society and international organizations [in the tens or hundreds of thousands]."

In August, El Salvador broke diplomatic relations with Taiwan to open them with China.

In October, Pope Francis canonized Archbishop Oscar Romero, who before his assassination used his pulpit to preach peace and to denounce state killings and abuses of power.

BROWSE COUNTRIES

Choose...

EXHIBIT '24':

Annual Report: El Salvador 2017/2018 – Amnesty International

AMNESTY INTERNATIONAL

EL SALVADOR 2017/2018

ANNUAL REPORT EL SALVADOR

← Back to El Salvador

EL SALVADOR 2017/2018

El Salvador's high rate of gender-based violence continued to make it one of the most dangerous countries to be a woman. A total ban on abortion persisted, and women were convicted of aggravated homicide after suffering miscarriages or other obstetric emergencies. To combat violence, the government implemented a series of security measures, which did not comply with human rights standards. Measures were taken to address impunity for historical abuses; however, the executive and legislative branches of government admitted being in contempt of a 2016 Supreme Court judgment that declared the 1993 Amnesty Law unconstitutional.

Background

El Salvador continued to have one of the world's highest murder rates, although the number of homicides fell from 5,280 in 2016 to 3,605 in 2017. The figure for 2017 included 429 femicides.

Women's rights

Abortion continued to be prohib. in all circumstances, and carried crimin. enalties for women and health care providers. Women from poor backgrounds were disproportionately affected.

In March, the Inter-American Commission on Human Rights (IACHR) admitted a petition in the case of Manuela, a woman convicted of homicide after having a miscarriage, and who died from cancer in prison while serving her sentence.

On 5 July, Evelyn Beatriz Hernández Cruz was sentenced to 30 years' imprisonment after being convicted on charges of aggravated homicide after suffering obstetric complications resulting in a miscarriage. On 13 December, a court denied the release of Teodora del Carmen Vásquez; she had suffered a stillbirth in 2007 and was later sentenced to 30 years for aggravated homicide.

In August a parliamentarian for the opposition Nationalist Republican Alliance presented a new proposal to decriminalize abortion in two circumstances: when a woman's life is at risk or when the pregnancy is a consequence of rape of a minor. The proposal remained pending in Parliament. This followed previous, unsuccessful attempts at partial decriminalization of abortion in 2016.

In August, Congress approved a law banning child marriage, without exceptions.

In November, the IACHR admitted a petition on the case of "Beatriz", a woman who in 2013 was denied an abortion despite her life being put at risk by the pregnancy, and the foetus being diagnosed with fatal impairment, which would not have allowed its survival after birth.

Human rights defenders

In June the home of human rights defender Sonia Sánchez Pérez was illegally searched by National Civilian Police officers. In 2015 the Office of the Human Rights Ombudsman had granted her precautionary measures for her environmental protection work.

Rights of lesbian, gay, bisexual, transgender and intersex people

In October, Karla Avelar, a human rights defender and founder of the first association of trans people in El Salvador, announced that she would claim asylum in Europe because of a lack of protection by the authorities, despite several security incidents, threats, and being the victim of extortion by criminal gangs. Between January and September, the Association for Communicating and Training Trans Women in El Salvador (COMCAVIS TRANS) reported 28 serious attacks, most of them murders, perpetrated against LGBTI people.[1]

Extrajudicial executions

In September the Human Rights Institute of José Simeón Cañas Central American University and the NGO Passionist Social Service reported before the IACHR that the armed forces and National Civilian Police were responsible for carrying out extrajudicial executions.

Police and security forces

In November the UN High Commissioner for Human Rights urged El Salvador to end the extraordinary security measures adopted since 2016 to combat gang violence and organized crime, which failed to comply with international human rights standards. The measures included prolonged and isolated detention under inhuman conditions, and prolonged suspension of family visits to prisoners.

Internally displaced people

On 6 and 13 October, for the first time, the Constitutional Chamber of the Supreme Court of Justice issued two injunctions (*amparo*) to protect internally displaced people. The injunctions included protective measures for a family that had been forcibly internally displaced due to rape, threats, beatings and harassment by a gang. The decision was welcomed by the IACHR and the UN Special Rapporteur on the human rights of internally displaced persons.

Impunity

Measures were adopted nationally and internationally to redress crimes under international law and punish perpetrators of human rights violations committed during El Salvador's armed conflict from 1980 to 1992.

In May, a court ordered the reopening of the case of Monseñor Óscar Arnulfo Romero y Galdámez, Archbishop of San Salvador, who was murdered in 1980 by a death squad while celebrating mass.

Following a judgment by the Supreme Court in 2016 in which the 1993 Amnesty Law was ruled to be unconstitutional, the Court held a hearing in July to determine what steps the government had taken to comply with the ruling. In that hearing, both the executive and legislative branches of government admitted to being in contempt of the ruling.

In September the government created a commission to search for people who were subjected to enforced disappearance during the armed conflict.

In November, the Supreme Cou[illegible] the USA cleared the way for Colonel In[illegible]ate Orlando Montano Morales to be tried in Spain on charges that he conspired in the killing of six Jesuit priests, their housekeeper and her daughter in El Salvador in 1989.

1. Americas: "No safe place" – Salvadorans, Guatemalans and Hondurans seeking asylum in Mexico based on their sexual orientation and/or gender identity (AMR 01/7258/2017)

EXHIBIT '25':

El Salvador Travel Advisory – U.S. Department of State (01/29/2019)

El Salvador Travel Advisory

Travel Advisory
January 29, 2019

El Salvador - Level 3: Reconsider Travel

Reconsider travel to El Salvador due to **crime**.

Violent crime, such as murder, assault, rape, and armed robbery, is common. Gang activity, such as extortion, violent street crime, and narcotics and arms trafficking, is widespread. Local police may lack the resources to respond effectively to serious criminal incidents.

Read the Safety and Security section on the country information page.

If you decide to travel to El Salvador:

- Be aware of your surroundings.
- Avoid walking or driving at night.
- Do not physically resist any robbery attempt.
- Be extra vigilant when visiting banks or ATMs.
- Do not display signs of wealth, such as wearing expensive watches or jewelry.
- Engage local guides certified by the national or local tourist authority when hiking in back country areas.
- Visit our website for Travel to High-Risk Areas.
- Enroll in the Smart Traveler Enrollment Program (STEP) to receive Alerts and make it easier to locate you in an emergency.
- Follow the Department of State on Facebook and Twitter.
- Review the Crime and Safety Report for El

Salvador.

- U.S. citizens who travel abroad should always have a contingency plan for emergency situations. Review the Traveler's Checklist.

Last Update: Reissued after periodic review without changes.

EXHIBIT '26':

El Salvador 2018 Human Rights Report – U.S. Department of State

EL SALVADOR 2018 HUMAN RIGHTS REPORT

EXECUTIVE SUMMARY

El Salvador is a constitutional multiparty republic. Municipal and legislative elections held in March were generally free and fair, according to international observers, although slow tabulation contributed to reporting delays. Free and fair presidential elections took place in 2014.

Civilian authorities failed at times to maintain effective control over security forces.

Human rights issues included allegations of unlawful killings of suspected gang members and others by security forces; forced disappearances by military personnel; torture by security forces; harsh and life-threatening prison conditions; arbitrary arrest and detention; lack of government respect for judicial independence; widespread government corruption; violence against women and girls that was infrequently addressed by the authorities, as well as security force violence against lesbian, gay, bisexual, transgender, and intersex individuals; and children engaged in the worst forms of child labor.

Impunity persisted despite government steps to dismiss and prosecute some in the security forces, executive branch, and justice system who committed abuses.

Organized criminal elements, including local and transnational gangs and narcotics traffickers, were significant perpetrators of violent crimes and committed acts of murder, extortion, kidnapping, human trafficking, intimidation, and other threats and violence directed against police, judicial authorities, the business community, journalists, women, and members of vulnerable populations.

Section 1. Respect for the Integrity of the Person, Including Freedom from:

a. Arbitrary Deprivation of Life and Other Unlawful or Politically Motivated Killings

There were no reports that the government or its agents committed politically motivated killings. There were reports, however, of security force involvement in extrajudicial killings of suspected gang members. As of July 31, the Office of the Human Rights Ombudsman (PDDH) announced it was investigating 22 complaints against police officers, prison guards, and personnel of the Attorney General's Office for such killings.

The case continued against nine police officers charged in September 2017 with aggravated homicide and concealment stemming from the killing of five persons. Three of the accused were members of the now decommissioned Police Reaction Group (GRP), and police claimed at the time of the events that the deaths were justified homicides.

On March 2, the Attorney General's Office appealed the September 2017 acquittal of five police officers for aggravated homicide charges in the 2015 killing of a man at a farm in San Blas, San Jose Villanueva. The judge had ruled that the prosecutors failed to prove which of the five officers was specifically responsible for firing the fatal shot and likewise failed to prove conspiracy. On May 4, the Fourth Appellate Court of Appeals confirmed it would retry the case.

On February 23, police authorities in coordination with INTERPOL arrested Jaime Ernesto Bonilla Martinez, who lived in Texas, for participating in at least eight homicides as part of an alleged extermination group operating in San Miguel. The group, composed of civilians, some of whom were alleged rival gang members, and retired and active members of the military and police, was purportedly responsible for murder-for-hire and targeted killings of alleged gang members in San Miguel. Funding for the extermination group reportedly came from Salvadoran citizens living abroad.

As of October 25, alleged gang members had killed 21 police officers. On August 21, the Organized Crime Court convicted 61 MS-13 members of homicide, extortion, illicit trafficking, and conspiracy to kill police officers, among other crimes.

b. Disappearance

There were reports alleging that members of security and law enforcement were involved in unlawful disappearances. Since March 2017 law enforcement agencies had not released data on disappearances, citing a discrepancy between data collected by police and the Attorney General's Office.

On March 7, the Constitutional Chamber of the Supreme Court ruled that the armed forces were responsible for investigating the disappearance of two 17-year-old boys in Ilopango in 2014. According to the court, seven soldiers detained and searched them, tied their hands with their shoelaces, and took them to Colonia Santa Maria, which was controlled by a rival gang. The two youths missed school that afternoon and were not seen thereafter. The case was ongoing.

In May 2017 a Sonsonate court convicted five soldiers of forced disappearance committed in 2014 and sentenced them to eight years' imprisonment. Their defense attorneys filed an appeal, and the case remained ongoing. In January the Constitutional Chamber found the military in contempt of their August 2017 order that the Ministry of Defense investigate and report on civilian deaths caused by the military.

On September 1 and in December 2017, the Constitutional Chamber issued two sentences in forced disappearance cases from 1982. The Constitutional Chamber determined that investigations should be carried out on the whereabouts of the victims and underlined the state's responsibility in ensuring an unobstructed investigation. The chamber noted that the Ministry of Defense and the chief of the joint chiefs of staff of the armed forces were uncooperative in the investigation.

As of October the attorney general had opened investigations into 12 instances of forced disappearance during the 1980-92 civil war.

c. Torture and Other Cruel, Inhuman, or Degrading Treatment or Punishment

The law prohibits such practices, but there were reports of violations. As of July 31, the PDDH received 18 complaints of torture or cruel or inhuman treatment by the National Civil Police (PNC), the armed forces, and other public officials.

On May 29, a court recommended that colonels Hector Solano Caceres and David Iglesias Montalvo, along with Lieutenant Colonel Ascencio Sermeno face charges for homicide, bribery, and conspiracy for ordering the torture of two men in 2016 in Apaneca. In 2017 six soldiers were convicted in the same case.

Prison and Detention Center Conditions

Prison and detention center conditions remained harsh and life threatening due to gross overcrowding, unhygienic conditions, and gang activities.

Physical Conditions: Overcrowding remained a serious threat to prisoners' health and welfare. As of June 30, the PDDH reported that think tank Salvadoran

Foundation for Economic and Social Development reported 38,849 inmates were being held in facilities designed for 18,051 inmates.

Convicted inmates and pretrial detainees were sometimes held in the same prison cells.

In June the Salvadoran Institute for Child Development (ISNA) reported 945 juveniles in detention, with 274 of those awaiting trial. Of those, 356 were held on homicide charges, 465 for extortion, 313 for drug-related crimes, and 143 for gang membership. As of July ISNA reported that three minors were killed by gang members while in detention, compared with nine in 2017. ISNA also reported that as of June, seven minors were victims of trafficking in persons, compared with 18 in 2017.

Gangs remained prevalent in prisons. As of September 2017, detention centers held 17,614 current or former gang members, or 46 percent of the prison population. So-called extraordinary measures were designed to interrupt gang communications and coordination between imprisoned leaders and gang members outside the prisons. Smuggling of weapons, drugs, and other contraband such as cell phones and cell phone SIM cards was reduced but remained a problem in the prisons, at times with complicity from prison officials.

Law enforcement officials credited the extraordinary measures with a 45 percent reduction in homicides. The PDDH and human rights groups faulted the measures for lacking judicial oversight. On August 16, the Legislative Assembly formalized some elements of the extraordinary measures as part of a reformed penitentiary code, which now allows supervised family visits.

In many facilities provisions for sanitation, potable water, ventilation, temperature control, medical care, and lighting were inadequate, according to the PDDH. From August 2017 to May, the General Prison Directorate reported 2,440 cases of inmate malnutrition and the PDDH reported more than 500 cases of severe malnutrition in Izalco and Ciudad Barrios prisons. The PDDH noted that in 2017 a total of 64 inmates died, some of them due to unspecified causes.

In October the PNC reported overcrowding in police holding cells, with 5,500 detainees in cells designed for 1,500 persons. Those in pretrial detention were held alongside sick inmates.

Administration: The PDDH has authority to investigate credible allegations of inhuman conditions. The Constitutional Chamber of the Supreme Court has authority over the protection of constitutional rights. The extraordinary measures granted broad authorities to wardens to order disciplinary actions, to include isolation and withholding family or religious visitations, without judicial oversight. Extraordinary measures ended in August when the Legislative Assembly reformed the penitentiary code.

Independent Monitoring: The government permitted visits by independent human rights observers, nongovernmental organizations (NGOs), and media to low- and medium-security prisons. Inspections of high-security prisons were limited to government officials, the PDDH, and the International Committee of the Red Cross (ICRC). Early in the year, the government reinstated the ICRC's access to all prisons. Church groups; the Institute for Human Rights at the University of Central America; lesbian, gay, bisexual, transgender, and intersex activists; the UN special rapporteur for extrajudicial, summary, or arbitrary executions; and other groups visited prisons during the year. The PDDH reported that from May 2017 to April, it conducted 1,644 unannounced prison inspections.

Improvements: Due to the construction of new prisons completed during the year and redistribution of prisoners, overcrowding declined from 334 percent to 215 percent as of August.

d. Arbitrary Arrest or Detention

Although the constitution prohibits arbitrary arrest and detention, there were numerous complaints that the PNC and military forces arbitrarily arrested and detained persons. As of July 31, the PDDH received 31 complaints of arbitrary detention, a decrease from 86 complaints received in the same period in 2017. NGOs reported that the PNC arbitrarily arrested and detained groups of persons on suspicion of gang affiliation. According to these NGOs, the accused were ostracized by their communities upon their return.

The law provides for the right of any person to challenge the lawfulness of his or her arrest or detention in court, and the government generally observed this provision.

Role of the Police and Security Apparatus

Arrest Procedures and Treatment of Detainees

The constitution requires a written warrant of arrest except in cases where an individual is caught in the act of committing a crime. Authorities apprehended persons with warrants based on evidence and issued by a judge. Police generally informed detainees promptly of charges against them.

The law permits release on bail for detainees who are unlikely to flee or whose release would not impede the investigation of the case. The bail system functioned adequately in most cases. The courts generally enforced a ruling that interrogation without the presence of counsel is coercive and that evidence obtained in such a manner is inadmissible. As a result, PNC authorities typically delayed questioning until a public defender or an attorney arrived. The constitution permits the PNC to hold suspects for 72 hours before presenting them to court. The law allows up to six months for investigation of serious crimes before requiring either a trial or dismissal of the case which may be extended by an appeals court. Many cases continued beyond the legally prescribed period.

Arbitrary Arrest: As of October 23, the PDDH reported 31 complaints of arbitrary detention or illegal detention, compared with 86 from January to August 2017.

Pretrial Detention: Lengthy pretrial detention was a significant problem. As of October, 30 percent of the general prison population was in pretrial detention. Some persons remained in pretrial detention longer than the maximum legal sentences for their alleged crimes. In such circumstances detainees may request a Supreme Court review of their continued detention.

e. Denial of Fair Public Trial

Although the constitution provides for an independent judiciary, the government did not always respect judicial independence, and the judiciary was burdened by inefficiency and corruption.

While the government generally respected court orders, some agencies ignored or minimally complied with orders, or sought to influence ongoing investigations. When ordered by the Constitutional Court on June 19 to release military records related to the El Mozote killings and serious civil war crimes, the Ministry of Defense responded it had already done so while denying investigators access to archival facilities at military bases, citing national security concerns. As of July

Arrest Procedures and Treatment of Detainees

The constitution requires a written warrant of arrest except in cases where an individual is caught in the act of committing a crime. Authorities apprehended persons with warrants based on evidence and issued by a judge. Police generally informed detainees promptly of charges against them.

The law permits release on bail for detainees who are unlikely to flee or whose release would not impede the investigation of the case. The bail system functioned adequately in most cases. The courts generally enforced a ruling that interrogation without the presence of counsel is coercive and that evidence obtained in such a manner is inadmissible. As a result, PNC authorities typically delayed questioning until a public defender or an attorney arrived. The constitution permits the PNC to hold suspects for 72 hours before presenting them to court. The law allows up to six months for investigation of serious crimes before requiring either a trial or dismissal of the case which may be extended by an appeals court. Many cases continued beyond the legally prescribed period.

Arbitrary Arrest: As of October 23, the PDDH reported 31 complaints of arbitrary detention or illegal detention, compared with 86 from January to August 2017.

Pretrial Detention: Lengthy pretrial detention was a significant problem. As of October, 30 percent of the general prison population was in pretrial detention. Some persons remained in pretrial detention longer than the maximum legal sentences for their alleged crimes. In such circumstances detainees may request a Supreme Court review of their continued detention.

e. Denial of Fair Public Trial

Although the constitution provides for an independent judiciary, the government did not always respect judicial independence, and the judiciary was burdened by inefficiency and corruption.

While the government generally respected court orders, some agencies ignored or minimally complied with orders, or sought to influence ongoing investigations. When ordered by the Constitutional Court on June 19 to release military records related to the El Mozote killings and serious civil war crimes, the Ministry of Defense responded it had already done so while denying investigators access to archival facilities at military bases, citing national security concerns. As of July

31, the Legislative Assembly had not complied with a 2015 ruling that it issue regulations to clarify certain sections of the political parties law regarding campaign contributions.

In a February 26 press conference, Minister of Defense David Munguia Payes criticized the attorney general's charges against three military officers after they were acquitted of obstruction of justice in a torture case. On February 27, UN Special Rapporteur on Extrajudicial, Summary, or Arbitrary Executions Agnes Callamard released a statement calling on Payes to respect the independence of the judiciary and reiterating her support for the attorney general. Media experts called Munguia's stagecraft menacing and reminiscent of civil war-era propaganda employed by the military junta.

While implemented to expedite fair trials, virtual trials still involved delays of up to eight months, according to a July 22 newspaper report. Virtual trials often involved group hearings before a judge, with defendants unable to consult with their defense lawyers in real time. The penitentiary code reforms passed in August allow defense lawyers to attend a hearing without the defendant's presence. Human rights groups questioned the constitutionality of the reform.

As of July 31, the PDDH received 31 complaints of lack of a fair, public trial.

Corruption in the judicial system contributed to a high level of impunity, undermining the rule of law and the public's respect for the judiciary. As of August 31, the Supreme Court heard 57 cases against judges due to irregularities, 52 of which remained under review; removed two judges; suspended nine others; and brought formal charges against eight judges. Accusations against judges included collusion with criminal elements and sexual harassment.

In 2016, in response to a petition by victims, a judge issued an order to reopen the investigation into the 1981 El Mozote massacre, in which an estimated 800 persons were killed. The PDDH concluded that the Attorney General's Office lacked initiative in investigating civil war crimes, The PDDH also cited the Attorney General Office's lack of cooperation from the Ministry of Defense and the Office of the President (CAPRES). On August 16, a group of Argentine forensics specialists testified they recovered 282 pieces of evidence determined to be human remains, including 143 skulls, 136 of them belonging to children younger than 12 years old. They also recovered 245 bullet casings corresponding to the type used in automatic weapons used by the armed forces.

Women who were accused of intentionally terminating their pregnancies were charged with aggravated homicide, but a number asserted they had suffered miscarriages, stillbirths and other medical emergencies during childbirth. Legal experts pointed to serious flaws in the forensics collection and interpretation.

In December 2017 Teodora del Carmen Vasquez' conviction on aggravated homicide charges was upheld by the same appeals judges who had earlier sentenced her to 30 years. The Supreme Court commuted her sentence on February 15, opining that the evidence and motive presented by the prosecution in the case was insufficient to support the charges.

During the first nine months of the year, the justice system released five women accused of aggravated homicide of their unborn or newborn children due to lack of evidence. Twenty-five other women remained in custody for infanticide.

Trial Procedures

The law provides for the right to a fair and public trial, and an independent judiciary generally enforced this right, although some trial court judges were subject to political and economic influence. By law juries hear only a narrow group of cases, such as environmental complaints. After the jury determines innocence or guilt, a panel of judges decides the sentence.

Defendants have the right to be present in court, question witnesses, and present witnesses and evidence. The constitution further provides for the presumption of innocence, the right to be informed promptly and in detail of charges, the right to a trial without undue delay, protection from self-incrimination, the right to communicate with an attorney of choice, the right to adequate time and facilities to prepare a defense, freedom from coercion, the right to appeal, and government-provided legal counsel for the indigent.

According to press reports, plea deals occurred in approximately 20 percent of cases, with the accused turning state's witness in order to prosecute others. Legal experts pointed to an overreliance on witness testimony in nearly all cases, as opposed to the use of forensics or other scientific evidence. The justice system lacked DNA analysis and other forensics capability. In criminal cases a judge may allow a private plaintiff to participate in trial proceedings (calling and cross-examining witnesses, providing evidence, etc.), assisting the prosecuting attorney in the trial procedure. Defendants have the right to free assistance of an interpreter. Authorities did not always respect these legal rights and protections.

Although a jury's verdict is final, a judge's verdict is subject to appeal. Trials are public unless a judge seals a case.

Political Prisoners and Detainees

There were no reports of political prisoners or detainees.

Civil Judicial Procedures and Remedies

The law provides for access to the courts, enabling litigants to bring civil lawsuits seeking damages for, as well as cessation of, human rights violations. Domestic court orders generally were enforced. Most attorneys pursued criminal prosecution and later requested civil compensation.

On May 25, the Constitutional Chamber declared unconstitutional Article 49 of the Civil Service Law, ruling that it violated the double jeopardy prohibition because previously established facts were taken as an essential element for a more serious administrative sanction.

f. Arbitrary or Unlawful Interference with Privacy, Family, Home, or Correspondence

The constitution prohibits such actions; however, a January news report claimed the state intelligence service tracked several journalists and collected compromising information about their private lives. The newspaper submitted photographic and whistleblower evidence to support its claim.

In many neighborhoods armed groups and gangs targeted certain persons; and interfered with privacy, family, and home life. Efforts by authorities to remedy these situations were generally ineffective.

Section 2. Respect for Civil Liberties, Including:

a. Freedom of Expression, Including for the Press

The constitution provides for freedom of expression, including for the press, and the government generally respected this right. The law permits the executive branch to use the emergency broadcasting service to take over all broadcast and cable networks temporarily to televise political programming.

Press and Media Freedom: There continued to be allegations that the government retaliated against members of the press for criticizing its policies. There were reports the Ministry of Labor conducted arbitrary labor inspections and financial audits of news organizations.

Both the Nationalist Republican Alliance (ARENA) and Farabundo Marti Liberation Front (FMLN) parties steered funding, including public funds, to journalists in exchange for positive coverage. The online news outlet *El Faro* reported during the year that former president Antonio Saca funneled $665,000 (currency is the U.S. dollar) to media contacts in exchange for positive coverage from 2004 until 2009, while former president Mauricio Funes continued the practice of using a secret fund to corrupt journalists from 2009 through 2014.

Violence and Harassment: On May 22, the Salvadoran Journalist Association (APES) reported that former youth secretary Carlos Aleman threatened *El Faro* journalist Gabriel Labrador after he published a report that accused Aleman of benefiting from illegal salary increases during the Saca administration. APES also reported that journalist Milagro Vallecillos received a call asking him where he would like a body disposed after he criticized the police investigation into the killing of journalist Karla Turcios.

In relation to reporting on the March 4 municipal and legislative assembly elections, APES recorded 15 complaints against civil servants, mayors, unions, and gang members. The incidents included three verbal threats, two physical assaults, one property damage claim, and three suspicious incidents. On March 19, online news outlet *Diario 1* journalist Miguel Lemus was physically attacked by members of the San Salvador city employees' union.

Minister of Defense Munguia reportedly visited media offices unannounced and accompanied by armed soldiers.

Censorship or Content Restrictions: Government advertising accounted for a significant portion of press advertising income. According to APES, media practiced self-censorship, especially in reporting on gangs and narcotics trafficking.

Nongovernmental Impact: APES noted journalists reporting on gangs and narcotics trafficking were subject to kidnappings, threats, and intimidation. Observers reported that gangs also charged print media companies to distribute in their communities, costing media outlets as much as 20 percent of their revenues.

Internet Freedom

The government did not restrict or disrupt access to the internet or censor online content, and there were no credible reports that the government monitored private online communications without appropriate legal authority.

The International Telecommunication Union reported 31 percent of the population used the internet in 2017.

Academic Freedom and Cultural Events

There were no government restrictions on academic freedom or cultural events.

b. Freedoms of Peaceful Assembly and Association

The constitution provides for the freedoms of peaceful assembly and association, and the government generally respected these rights.

c. Freedom of Religion

See the Department of State's *International Religious Freedom Report* at www.state.gov/religiousfreedomreport/.

d. Freedom of Movement

The constitution provides for freedom of internal movement, foreign travel, emigration, and repatriation. The government generally respected these rights, although in many areas the government could not guarantee freedom of movement due to criminal gang activity. As of July 31, the PDDH received two complaints of restrictions from freedom of movement, one against the PNC and the other against a court in Jiquilisco. Both cases involved subjects being detained without charge. The government cooperated with the Office of the UN High Commissioner for Refugees (UNHCR) and other humanitarian organizations in providing protection and some assistance to internally displaced persons, refugees, returning refugees, asylum seekers, stateless persons, and other persons of concern, although this was often difficult in gang-controlled neighborhoods.

In-country Movement: The major gangs controlled their own territory. Gang members did not allow persons living in another gang's controlled area to enter

Elections and Political Participation

Recent Elections: The most recent municipal and legislative elections occurred on March 4, with the final election results released by the Supreme Electoral Tribunal on March 20 and April 4, respectively. The election reports published by the Organization of American States and the EU electoral mission noted that the elections generally met international standards.

While the law prohibits public officials from campaigning in elections, this provision lacked consistent enforcement.

Participation of Women and Minorities: No laws limit participation of women or members of minorities in the political process, and they did participate.

Section 4. Corruption and Lack of Transparency in Government

The law provides criminal penalties for corruption by officials. While the Supreme Court investigated corruption in the executive and judicial branches, referring cases to the Attorney General's Office for possible criminal indictment, impunity remained endemic, with courts issuing inconsistent rulings and failing to address secret discretionary accounts within the government, for example in CAPRES.

Corruption: On September 12, a judge sentenced former president Antonio Saca to 10 years in prison. He originally faced up to 30 years in prison before seeking a plea deal. As part of his plea agreement, Saca detailed how he used a network of public officials and advisers to launder money into his ARENA political party, banks, media outlets, publicity companies, fronts, and other activities. Saca testified that weak institutions such as the Court of Accounts were ineffectual in conducting audits, with transparency mechanisms failing to detect fraud. While Saca's defense offered to return $15 million, the court found him fully liable and ordered him to repay $260 million and surrender his bank accounts and six companies managing 86 radio stations to the asset forfeiture program.

The attorney general investigated corruption pertaining to a discretionary fund within CAPRES in existence for more than 25 years and used by six presidents since 1989. It was originally created to provide resources for the national intelligence budget and CAPRES. The funds, totaling more than one billion dollars since its inception, had never been audited by the Court of Accounts. Both former presidents Saca and Funes were accused of embezzling more than $650 million from public funds. President Sanchez Ceren's discretionary account was

Elections and Political Participation

Recent Elections: The most recent municipal and legislative elections occurred on March 4, with the final election results released by the Supreme Electoral Tribunal on March 20 and April 4, respectively. The election reports published by the Organization of American States and the EU electoral mission noted that the elections generally met international standards.

While the law prohibits public officials from campaigning in elections, this provision lacked consistent enforcement.

Participation of Women and Minorities: No laws limit participation of women or members of minorities in the political process, and they did participate.

Section 4. Corruption and Lack of Transparency in Government

The law provides criminal penalties for corruption by officials. While the Supreme Court investigated corruption in the executive and judicial branches, referring cases to the Attorney General's Office for possible criminal indictment, impunity remained endemic, with courts issuing inconsistent rulings and failing to address secret discretionary accounts within the government, for example in CAPRES.

Corruption: On September 12, a judge sentenced former president Antonio Saca to 10 years in prison. He originally faced up to 30 years in prison before seeking a plea deal. As part of his plea agreement, Saca detailed how he used a network of public officials and advisers to launder money into his ARENA political party, banks, media outlets, publicity companies, fronts, and other activities. Saca testified that weak institutions such as the Court of Accounts were ineffectual in conducting audits, with transparency mechanisms failing to detect fraud. While Saca's defense offered to return $15 million, the court found him fully liable and ordered him to repay $260 million and surrender his bank accounts and six companies managing 86 radio stations to the asset forfeiture program.

The attorney general investigated corruption pertaining to a discretionary fund within CAPRES in existence for more than 25 years and used by six presidents since 1989. It was originally created to provide resources for the national intelligence budget and CAPRES. The funds, totaling more than one billion dollars since its inception, had never been audited by the Court of Accounts. Both former presidents Saca and Funes were accused of embezzling more than $650 million from public funds. President Sanchez Ceren's discretionary account was reportedly $147 million, while former presidents Saca and Funes controlled $301 million and $351, million respectively.

On June 19, the Attorney General's Office initiated an asset forfeiture claim against 24 properties owned by Funes, cabinet members, public officers, and his relatives. Properties included sugarcane plantations, beach houses, and homes.

As of July 31, the Ethics Tribunal reported it had received 190 complaints against 273 public officials. The tribunal sanctioned 20 public officials and forwarded six cases to the attorney general. The attorney general issued 28 arrest warrants on June 6, targeting individuals linked to more than $300 million allegedly embezzled by former president Funes from 2009 through 2014. Despite Constitutional Chamber restrictions on transferring funds without legislative approval, Funes allegedly had misdirected funding for personal gain since 2010. In July the attorney general accused Funes of using $215,000 in public funds to acquire 91 military-grade weapons through the Ministry of Defense for his personal use.

Financial Disclosure: The illicit enrichment law requires appointed and elected officials to declare their assets to the Probity Section of the Supreme Court. The law establishes fines for noncompliance that range from $11 to $571. The declarations were not available to the public unless requested by petition. In 2016 the Supreme Court established three criteria for selecting investigable cases: the age of the case (i.e., proximity to the statute of limitations), relevance of the position, and seriousness and notoriety of the alleged illicit enrichment.

Section 5. Governmental Attitude Regarding International and Nongovernmental Investigation of Alleged Abuses of Human Rights

A variety of domestic and international human rights groups generally operated without government restriction, investigating and publishing their findings on human rights cases. Although government officials generally were cooperative and responsive to these groups, officials expressed reluctance to discuss certain issues, such as extrajudicial killings and IDPs, with the PDDH.

Government Human Rights Bodies: The principal human rights investigative and monitoring body was the autonomous PDDH, whose head is nominated by the Legislative Assembly for a three-year term. The PDDH regularly issued advisory opinions, reports, and press releases on prominent human rights cases. The PDDH generally enjoyed government cooperation and was considered generally effective except on problems relating to criminal groups and gangs.

The PDDH maintained a constructive dialogue with CAPRES. The government publicly acknowledged receipt of reports, although in some cases it did not take action on recommendations, which are nonbinding. The PDDH faced threats, such as two robberies at its headquarters specifically targeting computers containing personally identifiable information.

Section 6. Discrimination, Societal Abuses, and Trafficking in Persons

Women

Rape and Domestic Violence: The law criminalizes rape of men or women, and the criminal code's definition of rape may apply to spousal rape, at the judge's discretion. The law requires the Attorney General's Office to prosecute rape cases whether or not the victim presses charges, and the law does not permit the victim to withdraw the criminal charge. The penalty for rape is generally imprisonment for six to 10 years. Laws against rape were not effectively enforced.

The law prohibits domestic violence and generally provides for sentences ranging from one to three years in prison, although some forms of domestic violence carry higher penalties. The law also permits restraining orders against offenders. Laws against domestic violence remained poorly enforced, and violence against women, including domestic violence, remained a widespread and serious problem. On July 31, the Salvadoran Organization of Women for Peace (ORMUSA) reported that in 2016 and 2017, only 5 percent of the 6,326 reported crimes against women went to trial. On July 4, police arrested a police commissioner for violating the terms of a restraining order protecting his spouse.

According to the World Health Organization, the rate of cases involving violence against women was 5,999 per 100,000 inhabitants and that 574 women were killed in 2015, 524 in 2016, and 469 in 2017.

Sexual Harassment: The law prohibits sexual harassment and provides imprisonment for five to eight years. Courts may impose fines in addition where the perpetrator maintains a position of trust or authority over the victim. The law mandates that employers take measures against sexual harassment and create and implement preventive programs. The government, however, did not enforce sexual harassment laws effectively.

On September 24, media reported the sole female member of an elite police unit was reassigned to a high threat precinct in retaliation for taking gender-discrimination claims to internal affairs inspectors. She said her uniforms were discarded, her sleeping quarters moved, and a colleague threatened to kill her.

Coercion in Population Control: There were no reports of coerced abortion or involuntary sterilization. (For more information on maternal mortality and availability of contraception, see Appendix C.)

Discrimination: The constitution grants women and men the same legal rights, but women did not enjoy equal pay or employment opportunities. The law establishes sentences of one to three years in prison for public officials who deny a person's civil rights based on gender and six months to two years for employers who discriminate against women in the workplace, but employees generally did not report such violations due to fear of employer reprisals.

On September 16, a labor union reported that a justice of the peace in Las Vueltas Chalatenango refused to promote a female clerk because she preferred a man have the position.

Children

Birth Registration: Children derive citizenship by birth within the country and from their parents. The law requires parents to register a child within 15 days of birth or pay a $2.85 fine. Failure to register resulted in denial of school enrollment.

Education: Education is free, universal, compulsory through the ninth grade, and nominally free through high school. Rural areas, however, frequently did not provide required education to all eligible students due to a lack of resources and because rural parents often withdrew their children from school by the sixth grade, requiring them to work.

Child Abuse: Child abuse remained a serious and widespread problem. The law gives children the right to petition the government without parental consent. Penalties for breaking the law include the child being taken into protective custody and three to 26 years' imprisonment, depending on the nature of the abuse.

On November 15, police arrested a woman in Juayua, Sonsonate, after she beat an 11-year-old child with a stick for losing a cell phone accessory. According to a

2016 National Health Survey, more than half of households punished their children physically and psychologically.

Early and Forced Marriage: The legal minimum age for marriage is 18. The law bans child marriage to prevent child abusers from using legal technicalities to avoid imprisonment by marrying their victims.

Sexual Exploitation of Children: Child sex trafficking is prohibited by law. Prison sentences for convicted traffickers stipulate imprisonment from six to 10 years. The minimum age for consensual sex is 18. The law classifies statutory rape as sexual relations with anyone younger than age 18 and includes penalties of four to 13 years' imprisonment for violations.

The law prohibits paying anyone younger than age 18 for sexual services. The law prohibits participating in, facilitating, or purchasing materials containing child pornography and provides for prison sentences of up to 16 years for violations. Despite these provisions, sexual exploitation of children remained a problem.

International Child Abductions: The country is a party to the 1980 Hague Convention on the Civil Aspects of International Child Abduction. See the Department of State's *Annual Report on International Parental Child Abduction* at https://travel.state.gov/content/travel/en/International-Parental-Child-Abduction/for-providers/legal-reports-and-data.html.

Anti-Semitism

The Jewish community totaled approximately 150 persons. There were no reports of anti-Semitic acts.

Trafficking in Persons

See the Department of State's *Trafficking in Persons Report* at www.state.gov/j/tip/rls/tiprpt/.

Persons with Disabilities

The law prohibits discrimination against persons with physical, sensory, intellectual, and mental disabilities. The National Council for Comprehensive Attention to Persons with Disability (CONAIPD), composed of representatives from multiple government entities, is the governmental agency responsible for protecting disability rights, but lacks enforcement power. According to CONAIPD, the government did not effectively enforce legal requirements for access to buildings, information, and communications for persons with disabilities. Few access ramps or provisions for the mobility of persons with disabilities existed.

According to CONAIPD, there is no mechanism to verify compliance with the law requiring businesses and nongovernment agencies to hire one person with disabilities for every 25 hires. CONAIPD reported employers frequently fired persons who acquired disabilities and would not consider persons with disabilities for work for which they qualified. Further, some academic institutions would not accept children with disabilities.

No formal system existed for filing a discrimination complaint involving a disability with the government.

Indigenous People

Indigenous communities reported they faced racial discrimination and economic disadvantage. According to community leaders, gangs pushed out of urban centers by police mounted incursions and appropriated indigenous land. They also reported gang members threatened their children for crossing gang territorial lines artificially drawn across ancestral indigenous land, forcing some children to drop out of school or leave home.

According to the 2007 census, the most recent for which this data was available, there were 60 indigenous groups, and 0.4 percent of citizens identified as indigenous, mainly from the Nahua-Pipl, Lencas, Cacaopera (Kakwira) and Maya Chorti groups. A 2014 constitutional amendment recognizes the rights of indigenous people to maintain their cultural and ethnic identitiy, but no laws provide indigenous people rights to share in revenue from exploitation of natural resources on historically indigenous lands. The government did not demarcate any lands as belonging to indigenous communities. Because few possessed title to land, opportunities for bank loans and other forms of credit remained limited.

While the law provides for the preservation of languages and archeological sites, it does not include the right to be consulted regarding development and other projects envisioned on their land.

Acts of Violence, Discrimination, and Other Societal Abuses Based on Sexual Orientation and Gender Identity

The law prohibits discrimination based on sexual orientation or gender identity, which also applies to discrimination in housing, employment, nationality, and access to government services. Gender identity and sexual orientation are included in the criminal code provisions covering hate crimes, along with race and political affiliation. NGOs reported that public officials, including police, engaged in violence and discrimination against sexual minorities. Persons from the lesbian, gay, bisexual, transgender, and intersex (LGBTI) community stated that the PNC, and the Attorney General's Office harassed transgender and gay individuals when they reported cases of violence against LGBTI persons, including by conducting strip searches.

As of July 31, the PDDH reported eight accusations made by the LGBTI community of five homicides, one unauthorized search, and one harassment complaint. The PDDH was unable to determine whether the incidents were bias-motivated. Activists also reported receiving death threats via social media; police generally failed to take action on these reports.

On April 16, the Ministry of Security and Justice led a formal signing ceremony for the Institutional Policy for the Protection of the LGBTI Community. A product of two years of roundtable dialogues, the policy instructs the security and migration sectors of government to consult with the Office of Secretariat for Social Inclusion to ensure LGBTI persons are treated in accordance with international standards in their interactions with the state. In November 2017 the Supreme Electoral Tribunal announced guidelines stating individuals cannot be denied the right to vote because the photograph on their identification card does not match their physical appearance.

HIV and AIDS Social Stigma

Although the law prohibits discrimination on the basis of HIV/AIDS status, Entre Amigos, an LGBTI NGO, reported discrimination due to HIV was widespread. As of July 31, the PDDH reported four cases of discrimination against persons with HIV or AIDS. This included use of pejorative language against an inmate by a prosecutor, denial of university access, lack of medical confidentiality in the prison system of an HIV-positive diagnosis and discriminatory treatment from other inmates, and discrimination by public-health caregivers to a child and her mother.

Section 7. Worker Rights

a. Freedom of Association and the Right to Collective Bargaining

The law provides the right of most workers to form and join independent unions, to strike, and to bargain collectively. The law also prohibits antiunion discrimination, although it does not require reinstatement of workers fired for union activity. Military personnel, national police, judges, and high-level public officers may not form or join unions. Workers who are representatives of the employer or in "positions of trust" also may not serve on the union's board of directors. The law does not define the term "positions of trust." The labor code does not cover public-sector workers and municipal workers, whose wages and terms of employment are regulated by the 1961 civil service law.

Unions must meet complex requirements to register, including having a minimum membership of 35. If the Ministry of Labor denies registration, the law prohibits any attempt to organize for up to six months following the denial. Collective bargaining is obligatory only if the union represents the majority of workers. Labor unions accused the ministry of trying to block the registration of unions not aligned with the government's party. Consequently, unions were unable to vote for membership in tripartite bodies, consisting of members of government, labor, and business.

The law contains cumbersome and complex procedures for conducting a legal strike. The law does not recognize the right to strike for public and municipal employees or for workers in essential services. The law does not specify which services meet this definition, and courts therefore apply this provision on a case-by-case basis. The law requires that 30 percent of all workers in an enterprise must support a strike for it to be legal and that 51 percent must support the strike before all workers are bound by the decision to strike. Unions may strike only to obtain or modify a collective bargaining agreement or to protect the common professional interests of the workers. They must also engage in negotiation, mediation, and arbitration processes before striking, although many groups often skipped or went through these steps quickly. The law prohibits workers from appealing a government decision declaring a strike illegal.

In lieu of requiring employers to reinstate illegally dismissed workers, the law requires employers to pay the workers the equivalent of 30 days of their basic salary for each year of service. The law specifies 30 reasons for which an employer can terminate a worker's contract without triggering any additional responsibilities, including consistent negligence, leaking private company information, or committing immoral acts while on duty. An employer may also legally suspend workers, including for reasons of economic downturn or market conditions. As of July the Ministry of Labor had received 1,778 complaints of violations of the labor code, including 565 instances of failure to pay the minimum wage.

The government did not effectively enforce the laws on freedom of association and the right to collective bargaining. Resources to conduct inspections remained inadequate, and remedies remained ineffective. Penalties for employers who fire workers with the goal or effect of ensuring the union no longer met the minimum number of members ranged from 10 to 50 times the monthly minimum salary. These were paid to the government's general fund, not to the fired employee. The penalty for employers who interfere with the right to strike was between $3,000 and $15,000. Such penalties remained insufficient to deter violations. The Ministry of Labor acknowledged it lacked sufficient resources, such as vehicles, fuel, and computers, to enforce the law fully. Judicial procedures were subject to lengthy delays and appeals. According to union representatives, the government inconsistently enforced labor rights for public workers, maquila/textile workers, food manufacturing workers, subcontracted workers in the construction industry, security guards, informal-sector workers, and migrant workers. As of July the ministry had received 15 claims of violations for labor discrimination.

On November 10, a court ordered a mayor in Conchagua to cease age discrimination of a group female employees. The employees filed a complaint with the Ministry of Labor that they were subjected to harassment by the mayor and his subordinates because of their age and his desire to replace them.

Unions functioned independently from the government and political parties, although many generally were aligned with the ARENA, FMLN, or other political parties. According to union leaders, the administration blacklisted public-sector employees who they believed were close with the opposition. Workers at times engaged in strikes regardless of whether the strikes met legal requirements. The International Labor Organization (ILO) Conference Committee on the Application of Standards discussed the country for the fourth year in a row over the nonfunctioning of the tripartite Higher Labor Council.

b. Prohibition of Forced or Compulsory Labor

The law prohibits all forms of forced or compulsory labor. The government generally did not effectively enforce such laws. The labor code's default fine of $57 per violation applied. This penalty was generally not sufficient to deter violations. The lack of sufficient resources for inspectors reduced their ability to enforce the law fully. The Ministry of Labor did not report on incidents of forced labor. Gangs subjected children to forced labor in illicit activities, including selling or transporting drugs (see section 7.c.).

Also see the Department of State's *Trafficking in Persons Report* at www.state.gov/j/tip/rls/tiprpt/.

c. Prohibition of Child Labor and Minimum Age for Employment

The law prohibits the employment of children younger than age 14. The law allows children between the ages of 14 and 18 to engage in light work if the work does not damage the child's health or development or interfere with compulsory education. The law prohibits children younger than age 16 from working more than six hours per day and 34 hours per week; those younger than age 18 are prohibited from working at night or in occupations considered hazardous. The Ministry of Labor maintained a list of the types of work considered hazardous and prohibited for children, to include repairing heavy machinery, mining, handling weapons, fishing and harvesting mollusks, and working at heights above five feet while doing construction, erecting antennas, or working on billboards. Children age 16 and older may engage in light work on coffee and sugar plantations and in the fishing industry so long as it does not harm their health or interfere with their education.

The Ministry of Labor maintains responsibility for enforcing child labor laws but did so with limited effectiveness. Child labor remained a serious and widespread problem. The law specifies a default fine of no more than $60 for each violation of most labor laws, including child labor laws; such penalties were insufficient to act as a deterrent. Labor inspectors focused almost exclusively on the formal sector. According to the ministry, from January 2017 through May, officials conducted 1,440 child labor inspections that discovered 18 minors, five of whom were unauthorized to work. By comparison, as of September 2017, according to the ministry, there were 140,700 children and adolescents working, of whom 91,257 were employed in "dangerous work" in the informal sector. No information on any investigations or prosecutions by the government was available. The ministry did not effectively enforce child labor laws in the informal sector.

There were reports of children younger than age 16 engaging in the worst forms of child labor, including in coffee cultivation, fishing, shellfish collection, and fireworks production. Children were subjected to other worst forms of child labor, including commercial sexual exploitation (see section 6, Children) and recruitment into illegal gangs to perform illicit activities related to the arms and drug trades, including committing homicide. Children were engaged in child labor, including domestic work, the production of cereal grains and baked goods, cattle raising, and vending. Orphans and children from poor families frequently worked as street vendors and general laborers in small businesses despite the presence of law enforcement officials.

Also see the Department of Labor's *Findings on the Worst Forms of Child Labor* at www.dol.gov/ilab/reports/child-labor/findings/.

d. Discrimination with Respect to Employment and Occupation

The constitution, labor laws, and state regulations prohibit discrimination regarding race, color, sex, religion, political opinion, national extraction (except in cases determined to protect local workers), social origin, gender, disability, language, or HIV-positive status. The government did not effectively enforce those laws and regulations. Sexual orientation and gender identity are not included in the constitution or labor law, although the PDDH and the Ministry of Labor actively sought to protect workers against discrimination on those grounds.

Discrimination in employment and occupation occurred with respect to gender, disability, and sexual orientation or gender identity (see sections 6 and 7.e.). According to the Ministry of Labor, migrant workers have the same rights as citizens, but the ministry did not enforce them.

On January 30, the Legislative Assembly reformed the labor code, prohibiting discriminatory practices and violence against women in the workplace. Further, on June 26, the Legislative Assembly reformed the labor code, civil service law, and the Vacations and Permits Law for Public Employees, prohibiting the dismissal of women returning from maternity leave for up to six months.

e. Acceptable Conditions of Work

There is no national minimum wage; the minimum wage is determined by sector. In January a major minimum wage increase went into effect that included increases of nearly 40 percent for apparel assembly workers and more than 100 percent for workers in coffee and sugar harvesting. After the increase the minimum daily wage was $10 for retail, service, and industrial employees; $9.84 for apparel assembly workers; and $3.94 for agricultural workers. The government reported the poverty income level was $179.67 per month in urban areas and $126.97 per month in rural areas.

The law sets a maximum normal workweek of 44 hours, limited to no more than six days and to no more than eight hours per day, but allows overtime, which is to be paid at a rate of double the usual hourly wage. The law mandates that full-time employees receive pay for an eight-hour day of rest in addition to the 44-hour normal workweek. The law provides that employers must pay double-time for work on designated annual holidays, a Christmas bonus based on the time of service of the employee, and 15 days of paid annual leave. The law prohibits compulsory overtime. The law states that domestic employees, such as maids and gardeners, are obligated to work on holidays if their employer makes this request, but they are entitled to double pay in these instances. The government did not adequately enforce these laws.

The Ministry of Labor is responsible for setting workplace safety standards, and the law establishes a tripartite committee to review the standards. The law requires employers to take steps to meet health and safety requirements in the workplace, including providing proper equipment and training and a violence-free environment. Employers who violate most labor laws could receive a default fine of no more than $57 for each violation. While the laws were appropriate for the main industries, a lack of compliance inspectors led to poor enforcement. These penalties were also insufficient to deter violations, and some companies reportedly found it more cost effective to pay the fines than to comply with the law. The law promotes occupational safety awareness, training, and worker participation in occupational health and safety matters.

The Ministry of Labor is responsible for enforcing the law. The government proved more effective in enforcing the minimum wage law in the formal sector than in the informal sector. Unions reported the ministry failed to enforce the law for subcontracted workers hired for public reconstruction contracts. The government provided its inspectors updated training in both occupational safety and labor standards. As of June the ministry conducted 13,315 inspections, in addition to 3,857 inspections to follow up with prior investigations, and had levied $777,000 in fines against businesses.

Allegations of corruption among labor inspectors continued. The Labor Ministry received complaints regarding failure to pay overtime, minimum wage violations, unpaid salaries, and cases of employers illegally withholding benefits (including social security and pension funds) from workers.

Reports of overtime and wage violations existed in several sectors. According to the Labor Ministry, employers in the agriculture sector did not generally grant annual bonuses, vacation days, or days of rest. Women in domestic service and the industrial manufacturing for export industry, particularly in the export-processing zones, faced exploitation, mistreatment, verbal abuse, threats, sexual harassment, and generally poor work conditions. Workers in the construction industry and domestic service reportedly fell subject to violations of wage, hour, and safety laws. According to ORMUSA, apparel companies violated women's rights through occupational health violations and unpaid overtime. There were reports of occupational safety and health violations in other sectors, including reports that a very large percentage of buildings were out of compliance with safety standards set by the General Law on Risk Protection. The government proved ineffective in pursuing such violations.

In some cases the country's high crime rate negatively affected acceptable conditions of work as well as workers' psychological and physical health. Some workers, such as bus drivers, bill collectors, messengers, and teachers in high-risk areas, reported being subject to extortion and death threats.

As of July the Ministry of Labor reported 5,199 workplace accidents. These included 2,609 accidents in the services sector, 1,859 in the industrial sector, 620 in the commercial sector, and 111 in the agricultural sector. The ministry did not report any deaths from workplace-related accidents.

Workers may legally remove themselves from situations that endanger health or safety without jeopardy to their employment, but authorities lacked the ability to protect employees in this situation effectively.

CERTIFICATE OF SERVICE

Re: Wuiliam Edgardo CALDERON-ESPINOZA - A206-897-574
Sandra Liseth LOPEZ DE CALDERON - A206-897-567
Willian Edgardo CALDERON-LOPEZ - A206-897-565
Katherine Rodelmy CALDERON-LOPEZ - A206-897-566

I, Christopher A. Reed, hereby certify that I am a resident of or employed in the County of Los Angeles, State of California over 18 years of age, not a party to the within action and that I am employed at and my business address is:

Law Offices of Brian D. Lerner, APC
3233 E. Broadway
Long Beach, CA 90803
Telephone: (562) 495-0554
Facsimile: (562) 608-8672

On July 18, 2019, I served a copy of the attached ***SUPPLEMENTAL DOCUMENTS FOR APPLICATION FOR ASYLUM, WITHHOLDING OF REMOVAL AND PROTECTION UNDER THE CONVENTION AGAINST TORTURE*** on the following person(s) by the following method(s):

Office of the Assistant Chief Counsel
Department of Homeland Security
606 S. Olive Street, 8th Floor
Los Angeles, CA 90014
(iceeservice@ice.dhs.gov)

I declare under penalty of perjury that the foregoing is true and correct. Executed in Long Beach, California.

DATED: July 18, 2019

By: ____________
Christopher A. Reed
Attorney at Law

ABOUT THE AUTHOR

Brian D. Lerner is an Immigration Lawyer and runs a National Immigration Law Firm for nearly 30 years. He is an attorney who is a certified specialist that might help in Immigration & Nationality Law as issued by the California State Bar, Board of Legal Specialization. Attorney Lerner is an expert in Immigration Law, Removal and Deportation, Citizenship, Waiver and Appeals.

He has been a licensed attorney since 1992 and started the Law Offices of Brian D. Lerner, APC. The immigration practice consists of Immigration and Nationality Law, and everything involved with and regarding immigration which includes citizenship, investment visas, family and employment visas, removal and deportation hearings, appeals, waivers, adjustment, consulate processing and all types of immigration and citizenship matters.

He has represented clients from all over the U.S. and in many countries around the world. One side of his practice is dedicated to keeping people in the U.S. and fighting for their immigration rights, while another side is to get people back who have been deported and removed from the U.S.

Also, there is the affirmative part of Immigration Law which Brian Lerner has helped numerous people come into the U.S. on business visas, investment visas, student visas, fiancée and marriage visas, religious visas and many more. Attorney Lerner has helped immigrants who are victims of crime and domestic violence or ones that are married to abusers.

In other words, Attorney Lerner has a firm that helps people all over the U.S. He has dedicated significant time to preparing numerous petitions and applications for you to get at a fraction of the price of hiring an attorney. He says it is the next best thing to a real attorney because they are real petitions prepared by an expert.

www.ingramcontent.com/pod-product-compliance
Lightning Source LLC
Chambersburg PA
CBHW051754200326
41597CB00025B/4554